Our Family Business Crisis

Our Family Business Crisis and How It Made Us Stronger

Wayne Rivers

Published by The Family Business Institute Inc.
4050 Wake Forest Road, Suite 110
Raleigh, North Carolina 27609
877-326-2493
www.familybusinessinstitute.com
www.ourfamilybusinesscrisis.com

This book is written as a general narrative and is not a substitute for individualized, professional advice. Readers should use their own judgment and consult reputable advisers for specific applications to family business needs and challenges.

The author has made every effort to ensure the accuracy and completeness of information contained in this book; however, the author assumes no responsibility for errors, inaccuracies, omissions, or inconsistencies herein. Any slights of people, places, or organizations are unintentional. The Dobach family case study is a fictional composite of many of the individuals, families, businesses, and situations with which The Family Business Institute Inc. has worked over the years. The individuals and situations in this book are representations only and are not in any way intended to represent any particular individual, family, or business.

Family business members and employees can be either male or female. Unless the context is specifically feminine, we decided to use the masculine pronoun throughout simply because we desired to avoid cumbersome language (he/she, his/her, etc.). We mean no discrimination, bias, or prejudice with respect to gender.

ISBN-13: 9780692659168
ISBN-10: 0692659161
Library of Congress Control Number: 2016935769
Family Business Institute, The, Raleigh, NC

Early March 2014

The founder of our company wielded the old cliché about death and taxes frequently—he always cackled wickedly when he said it—and we had experienced plenty of both during our three generations in business. What threatened to take us down, however, was neither death nor taxes, but change. In 2014, we were whipsawed by a number of changes that we did not foresee. Thank goodness we were able to rally as a family, put our egos aside, and make the tough decisions we needed to make. It wasn't easy, but had we not undertaken some serious evaluation and introspection…well, I wouldn't be telling this story.

This book is an exploration of that critical period of time in our family business, how we reacted to the abrupt and unsettling changes that threatened us, and some of the decisions, tools, processes, and techniques we used to push forward, survive, and eventually prosper again as both a harmonious family and a healthy business.

The place to start is the critical juncture when our banker unexpectedly called a meeting with our owners. We had done business with First National, our hometown bank, almost from the day Leon Dobach, the family patriarch and founder of the company, started Dobach Mechanical. Our current banker, Barney Smith, had worked with us for well over a decade. He was in the same Rotary club with Fred, Leon's son and president of the company, and went to the same church as Velma, Fred's sister who ran company administration and her husband Arthur. To us, it was a given that our relationship with Barney and First National went deeper than just black and white, dollars and cents. Then we had that fateful meeting.

Fred, Velma, and Casey, the youngest of Leon's children who ran the business development part of operations, met with Barney bright and early on a cold, rainy Tuesday morning. There was little of the normal lighthearted social banter. Barney got right down to brass tacks.

"Folks," he said, "I'm sorry to have to be the bearer of bad news. Lord knows I'm the last guy to want to darken your doorway with this sort of thing. But we at First National have a serious problem, and I have to bring this to your attention in the clearest possible terms. Things have obviously changed at Dobach Mechanical since the recession started in 2008. You've had several negative or barely break-even years in a row, and currently there isn't a lot of evidence things are getting better. Generations Real Estate appears to be a real drain on Dobach Mechanical and the rest of the family properties. We're worried that the capital calls you've had on the Florida investment and the low margins at Dobach Mechanical have put the whole enterprise in jeopardy. Frankly, we're not sure your financials accurately reflect the company's true financial health."

"You know our volume has almost returned to its prerecession level, right?" Fred said evenly.

"We do, Fred, of course, and that's positive. It's just there is little margin in the work you have taken on, and this soft patch you've been in has caused your ratios to suffer and your working capital to drop precipitously. As it stands today, you're awfully close to being out of compliance with your loan covenants. A few bad jobs and—"

Barney opened his hands and shrugged in a gesture of uncertainty.

Casey blurted out, "Just hold on one damn minute, Smith! Sure, Generations has had some trouble—I'm the first to admit that. But our managing partner says we're out of the woods, and South Florida real estate is on the way back. We shouldn't have any more trouble down there; there should be smooth sailing ahead. I don't know why suddenly you're so worked up!"

Barney said, "Casey, you might be right, but from a lender standpoint we are very concerned and feel that, between the issues at Dobach and Generations, we're in a very vulnerable position as your bank. We can't let the numbers slip past what the covenants require; that's why I'm here. To be blunt, we just don't think that Generations has any real value at all, and it represents a serious threat to everything you have built in your and your father's lifetimes."

The group exchanged worried glances.

He continued. "I have one other piece of news for you."

"Wow, Barney, is there another shoe to drop?" Velma asked.

"Maybe. We're not entirely sure, but there could be. As you know, the bank has invested big money in IT in the past few years, and that has allowed us to beef up our fraud department. Our system has sent up several red flags on your account. We don't know about some payments we're seeing coming through. This is a fairly recent development, but the checks are pretty regular. We're concerned that something, ah, irregular might be taking place."

Casey's mouth fell open in surprise.

Velma asked, "What are you saying, Barney? Has someone got his hand in the cookie jar?" She glanced over at Casey, who averted his eyes.

"Don't get me wrong, Velma. We're not accusing anyone of anything. I'm just suggesting that you ought to look into this and make sure that everybody is observing normal procedures for check writing and invoice approval. We've had far too many of our small business clients get taken advantage of by people they trust. It could be nothing at all, just an old banker worrying unnecessarily. But it is definitely worth looking into."

Looking at Barney, Fred said, "It's probably nothing. I'm sure there's a simple answer. We'll look into it."

"Thanks, Fred. Please keep in mind, all of you, that that's not the biggest issue. The big one is that, due to poor cash flows and the problem real estate, Dobach Mechanical might in reality have a net worth approaching zero. We bankers tend to be awfully conservative when looking at numbers, but the reality is that, given everything that's taken place since 2008, the company might not have enough reserves to meet its loan covenants, and we are being forced to review your file very carefully. Ultimately, the softening financials we're seeing might force us to call your loans and operating line of credit."

Rising to his feet, Casey exploded. "That's bullshit, Smith! Our dad started with your bank in the 1950s, and for you to come in here and threaten us this way is absolutely unprofessional! We've never so much as been late on one loan payment, and we've always been among your best customers in this town. For you to sit here and have the balls to talk to us this way makes me sick to my stomach! If I had my way, I'd pick you up and throw you out on your ass right now!"

"Hold your water, Casey," Fred said lifting both hands in an effort to soothe his furious younger brother. "Barney is just doing his job. I know when we look into everything we'll be able to demonstrate that Dobach Mechanical is as strong as ever and that all this is just a misunderstanding based on overabundant caution."

Casey thumped back into his seat with a scowl.

"We hope you're right, Fred. But here's the bank's position. You need to get together and present a business plan for how you're going to increase Dobach Mechanical's cash flows, net worth, and working capital. We're not going to pull your line of credit willy-nilly. But the regulators are putting pressure on us, and that means we have to put pressure on you to get your credit healthier. You all need to have a solid business plan in writing to us in the next ninety days, or we might be forced to take more drastic action."

"I've heard enough of this crap," Casey muttered. As he shoved his chair away from the table and stormed out of the room, Fred looked at Velma and rolled his eyes. Barney seemed alarmed at Casey's vivid display of anger.

"What do you mean we need to have something in writing to present to the bank?" Velma asked. "We've never really had to do this before, so it's important to know specifically what you're requiring."

Barney explained, "We need to see realistic financial projections in a formal business plan. We want to know how specifically you're going to improve the current and future prospects for Dobach Mechanical and Generations Real Estate. The bank isn't here to recommend specifically what you are supposed to do, whether it's reducing expenses or selling assets or anything else. All we're saying is that you need to present a plan to put the company back on a sounder financial footing. We want to continue to do business with you, but you have to meet us halfway."

Fred said, "I'm not exactly sure where to start. But we'll get Amos on it right away, and we'll get all this put to bed. I bet in six months' time, Barney, we'll be joking and laughing that we ever had this meeting at all."

"I hope you're right, Fred. I'm sorry to have to be the bearer of bad tidings. We're looking forward to seeing a plan from you, and we also hope we can get all this set aside. Thanks for your time this morning."

With that, the meeting adjourned, and Barney left the conference room.

Velma looked at Fred, her eyes as big as saucers. "If the bank pulls our operating line of credit, we're going to have a pretty major issue with keeping things going. And what about the bonding company?"

"Yeah, that would be a helluva problem. I hope we can get this issue squared away before they get involved. We're going to have to roll up our sleeves and figure out how to create a business plan. I hope Amos has a handle on how to do one; I sure don't."

Seeking direction, Velma inquired, "What do you think we should do first, Fred?"

"I don't know exactly where to start, but I'll get Amos up to speed right away. And we should probably call a family meeting to let everybody know what's going on. The kids are all adults now, and they need to learn that running a family business isn't always a bed of roses. I'd hate for one of them to hear through the grapevine the company was in trouble. They ought to hear what the situation is from us rather than hearing it from a competitor or a gossip. Damn, this is no way to start a day!"

"No, it's not," Velma agreed. "I'll arrange to get everybody together this afternoon."

"Thanks, Vel. And you might want to talk to Casey and let him know that he needs to be on his best behavior and not flying off the handle like he did this morning. That won't help anything."

"OK, I'll talk to him. I've spent all these years cleaning up behind Casey; I guess I'm pretty good at it by now."

11

Early March 2014

First National had gotten our attention! We knew we hadn't fully recovered from the recession, but we felt we were gradually heading in the right direction. And now this! In order to make sense of our story, it is probably wise at this point to backtrack and provide context. The following is a short history of the business, introductions of the family and key nonfamily managers, and a brief look at the Dobach family's business interests.

Leon Dobach was born in 1926. His parents were small farmers in Virginia. Some of his earliest memories were of the deprivations of the Great Depression. The fact that his family's farm was so self-sufficient allowed them to weather those terrible times easier than most; however, Leon frequently told stories of those lean years and was as thrifty a human being as you can imagine!

Leon finished high school, declined to work for his dad on the family farm—apparently they butted heads regularly—and went to town to work as a helper for Mr. Johnson, a man who taught Sunday school at Leon's church, in his mechanical contracting and plumbing company. Due to his intelligence and hard work, Leon quickly vaulted his way up to project manager.

In 1952, he was drafted into the US Army for service in Korea. He returned home in 1954, and in 1955, even though he was very close to Mr. Johnson and appreciative of the opportunity he'd provided, Leon decided he'd had enough of working for other people.

Recognizing that his region of Virginia was growing, he saw an opportunity to open his own mechanical contracting company.

Leon's wife, Myra, in spite of her protests, became the company's first administrative and financial employee, and she kept the company books while juggling the responsibilities of raising three energetic children: Fred, Velma, and Casey. Leon worked very long hours and the company prospered, but he wasn't around much when his kids were young. The business was his passion and "firstborn child."

Even in "retirement," Leon still came to the office every day. He was famous for his continual mantra: "Ain't nothin' certain in life 'cept for death and taxes!" He rolled out that old saw anytime an employee asked about next year's raise or a concerned friend asked him about his health, and then he'd laugh delightedly as if he'd just coined the joke. In the end, he died quietly in his sleep at age eighty-one after a brief illness.

In 2014, Myra, age eighty-seven, lived in an assisted-care facility and was experiencing signs of dementia. Fred and Velma were faithful visitors and looked after their mom as she once cared for them. Myra never took to the business and got out of her bookkeeping role as soon as it was feasible. She appreciated the wealth, comfort, and lifestyle the company's success provided, but she resented the fact that the business always came first to Leon and everything else a distant second. She counseled her three children to keep their distances from the company and pay attention to their individual, family, and spiritual needs. Myra's main focus was her children and extended family. She thought that Leon's life's work, the business, was strong enough to survive him. She worried that her life's work, the family, wasn't as strong and that, without her as the "glue," the family would gradually fall apart.

Leon and Myra's oldest child was Fred. At sixty-four years old, he served as president of Dobach Mechanical Contracting Inc., a company with about $55 million in revenue. Fred had come to work with Leon in 1974 after his graduation from college, and he was very much his father's philosophical heir when it came to money and running the company. Even after Leon died, Fred continually referred to his father's philosophies and unwritten rules as the guidelines for how the company should be managed. Fred usually saw the glass as half empty and often wore a grim, worn-out expression. He was conservative in his views and manner of dress. He usually left the office at 4:00 p.m. and headed home to a few cocktails, an early dinner, and watching television. Other than the occasional round of golf at the country club, Fred had no hobbies outside of work.

Fred's wife, Daphne, was a homemaker and volunteer. She was also a worrier and a reactionary. For a few years in the 1990s, she managed a small five-employee business that she and Fred bought, and she hated almost every minute of it. That negative experience formed how she viewed the family firm and business in general. It was her belief that businesses existed to employ people, but all the talk of profit, productivity, and accountability was unrealistic, put loads of pressure on everyone, and bordered on immoral. Because her son Jack was so self-sufficient and capable, Daphne tended to focus her attention on her younger son Tyler and advocated for him whenever she perceived he needed her protection—which was fairly often.

Velma, Leon and Myra's second born, was vice president of administration and human resources at Dobach Mechanical. She was an attractive and stylish woman. Although a stickler for details, she was good with people and was generally well liked by her employees. She adored her only child Addie and worked closely with her, and because she worried about Addie's tepid devotion to motherhood, she saw that her three grandchildren had the maternal and material things they wanted.

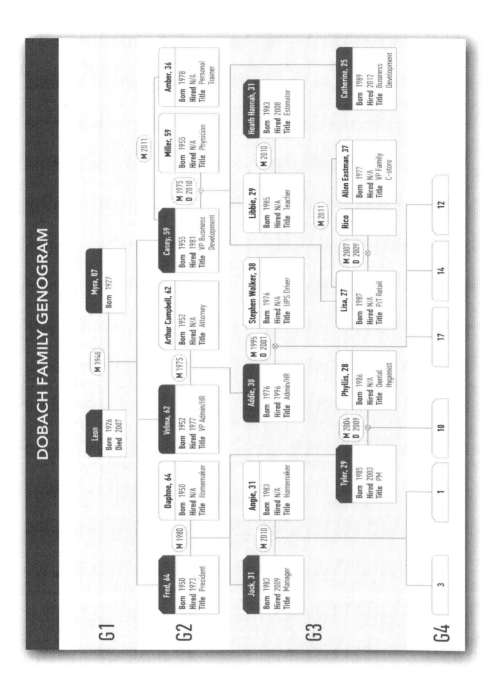

Velma had married Arthur Campbell in 1975, an attorney in general practice. Arthur was cut from the same cloth as the television lawyer Matlock: a little bit of a potbelly, a thick head of gray hair, and seersucker suits. He had an overall look of prosperity. Between Velma's compensation of $175,000 per year (Fred, Velma, and Casey were paid the same irrespective of their roles or tenure in the company at Leon and Myra's insistence, and they had never seen fit to revisit that decision) and Arthur's income as a successful attorney, they had the most comfortable lifestyle of the three siblings. They owned a large, well-appointed beach house where they enjoyed long weekends.

Casey, the youngest sibling, was born the year Leon started the business and served as vice president of business development. Casey was larger-than-life. He was big, boisterous, and a terrific four-sport high school athlete. His on-the-field talents were good enough to earn him a college football scholarship at a midsize school in spite of his indifferent performance in the classroom, and he got a fair amount of playing time as an offensive linemen. Casey was now about 125 pounds over his playing weight; tended to wear blue jeans, boat shoes, and short-sleeve shirts; and was always the life of the party. He loved to hunt, fish, and play golf, and his role as VP of business development lent itself to him being involved in lots of social and civic events without having to be chained to his desk. Leon had often complained that Casey spent so much time slapping backs, telling stories, buying drinks, and schmoozing that he forgot that the job of business development was to develop business for Dobach Mechanical.

There had been a family scandal a few years ago, when Casey began what he thought was a clandestine affair with his personal trainer, Amber, who was over twenty years younger. He eventually divorced Miller, the mother of his three daughters, and married Amber as soon as the divorce was final. The affair, divorce, and remarriage gave plenty of ammunition to the local gossips and scandalized the family.

Amber was nothing like Casey's first wife or any of the other women in the family. She had only a high school education and chose to wear clothing that might best be described as "clingy." She tried hard to fit into the family—probably too hard. She would assert herself in inappropriate places and, when her comments or observations were met with coolness or dismissed, she had emotional meltdowns. She, like Casey, loved parties and had a cocktail in her hand as soon as possible after quitting time. Adding fuel to the family scandal was the fact that Amber, at age thirty-six, was only seven years older than Casey's oldest daughter Libbie.

Turning to the third generation (G3) of the family, Fred and Daphne had two children, Jack and Tyler. Jack was the stereotypical, all-American oldest child. He was an obedient, attentive son who never rocked the boat and was an outstanding student. Jack got his undergraduate degree and then moved on to Wharton Business School, where he earned an MBA in finance. Following Wharton, he went to work for an investment bank on Wall Street at a starting salary of well over six figures. However, the financial meltdown of 2008 caused the firm to downsize and cost Jack, as a relatively new hire, his job.

Jack was thin, edgy, and always appeared to be deep in thought. In 2009 he returned to the less fast-paced and glamorous world of mechanical contracting at Dobach Mechanical, and because he'd earned so much in his previous job, the senior generation decided to compensate him at $120,000 a year. However, there really wasn't a place for Jack in the company; he had no title, no clearly defined role or job, no direct reports, and little guidance from Fred, Velma, or Casey. Everyone expected big things from him, but nobody, including Jack, knew exactly where he was supposed to start.

Jack's wife Angie, whom he'd met at Wharton, was a fast-track manager in a multinational company. Although separated by a long distance after graduation, she and Jack maintained the romance they had kindled in business school, and when Jack found himself changing careers and moving back to the family hometown, it sounded appealing to Angie, who had become disillusioned with big-business politics, constant pressure, and never-ending travel. They were married in 2010 and had the first of their two children in 2011. As if keeping up with two toddlers wasn't enough, Angie did CrossFit every morning to burn off some of her tremendous energy. She was very smart and insightful, and Jack considered her excellent business counsel.

Tyler, twenty-nine, was Fred and Daphne's younger son. Tyler worked for the company as a project manager. He'd attended college, but had had, like many kids, difficulty coping with the many temptations available to a twenty-something away from home for the first time. He failed to finish college—much to Fred's chagrin. Possibly as a result of the alcohol and drug issues that had required three stints in rehab, Tyler looked older than his brother. He was habitually rumpled and sloppy in appearance, and his hair stuck out in weird angles. As an employee, Tyler was predictably unpredictable. Over his ten years with Dobach, he'd had a few notable successes; however, his projects were just as likely to be disasters as home runs. There didn't seem to be any way to predict his performance. He was creative and talented, but he was also habitually late, disorganized, and inattentive to details, and had difficulty finishing things he started. Tyler had been married to a dental hygienist, but they divorced after five years, and his ex-wife had custody of their ten-year-old son.

Velma and Arthur had one child, Addie, thirty-eight. Velma continually looked out for Addie; to her mom, she could do no wrong. Among the G3 family, she had the longest tenure in the business, having come aboard in 1996 at age twenty. She worked for Velma in admin/HR/finance and earned $42,000 a year. Addie always seemed to be down and depressed. She was a heavy smoker, was overweight, and wore long, flowing garments to disguise her bulk. She tended to argue with others in both business and family settings. She'd married Stephen Walker, a UPS driver, in 1995, and they had three children ages seventeen, fourteen, and twelve. She and her husband had divorced after a ten-year marriage, and they shared custody of the children. Velma helped out with the youngsters quite a bit and was a virtual second mother; she fretted that Addie had just never had much maternal instinct. Addie suffered from type 2 diabetes as well as a variety of other health issues.

Casey had three children: Libbie, twenty-nine, Lisa, twenty-seven, and Catherine, twenty-five. Libbie was a teacher with a master's degree in English literature. She taught elementary school and tended to be "artsy." She loved to paint, sculpt, perform in local theater productions, and write in her journal. She was married to Heath, who had settled in comfortably at Dobach Mechanical as an estimator. Libbie had no interest whatsoever in athletics or any kind of physical activity, unlike her husband, who was a sports nut and who had himself been an excellent athlete as a young man. Both Libbie and Heath tended to be quiet and keep their heads down when controversial or business topics arose.

Lisa was Casey's middle child. She worked part-time at a friend's retail store and was very stylish, fit, and high energy. Lisa always had a smile on her face and was warm and welcoming; she had a unique talent for making everyone she encountered feel special. She was married to Allen, ten years her senior, who was a vice president in his family's successful convenience store business. Allen, like Jack and Angie, had an MBA. He had not served in the military, but you'd never know it to look at him. He had very short hair, angular features, and was a rail-thin long-distance runner. Allen had a great interest in the ebbs and flows of the fortunes of Dobach Mechanical since he experienced some of the same in his own family business. G3 often looked to Allen for his wisdom and insight into family business issues.

Casey's youngest child, Catherine, was the newest family member to enter the business, having joined in 2012. Catherine worked with her dad in business development and was showing an amazing alacrity for business. Her intelligence was off the charts. She was beautiful, with long blond hair, and wore fashionable, cutting-edge clothing. Because of her looks, it was easy to underestimate her intelligence and ambition, and some employees as well as family members tended not to take her very seriously. She was respectful of the generational hierarchy in the family business and tended to say comparatively little at family or business meetings. When she spoke, however, she was able to paraphrase complex discussions and situations into a tight, on-point, concise analytical package.

There were two "business family" members, or key employees, of note. Larry Brown, sixty-nine, was the company's general manager. He'd started with Leon the same year as Fred, 1974. Larry had only a high school education, but he had a terrific mind and was born for the mechanical contracting business. He'd been Leon's go-to guy, had forty years of tenure, and in Leon's eyes, had always been Fred's superior as a businessman. Employees, customers, and professionals with whom the company worked absolutely adored Larry. He was a big bear of a man with huge hands, a full head of silver hair, and a hearty laugh. He had been an asset to the company from the minute he came aboard, and although he was slowing down at age sixty-nine, he continued to be a tremendous contributor.

The other business-family member was Amos Lee, sixty-six. Amos's title was controller, and he'd arrived at Dobach Mechanical in 1989. He was pale and bookish, and wore thick glasses. Amos combed his hair from one side to the other in a vain attempt to hide his growing baldness. He was a creature of habit. He arrived at work precisely at 8:00 a.m. each day, prepared his coffee, fired up his computer, worked quietly, and left precisely at 5:00 p.m. Amos rarely spoke to others in the company unless they engaged him first. He was anal about establishing and enforcing policies, rules, and regulations. Because of his affinity for noting whenever anyone broke one of his precious rules, the employees didn't care for him very much. Although Velma was technically Amos's supervisor, she tended to keep her distance. Fred worked the closest with him and was usually his biggest supporter.

There were three primary business entities. The first, the goose that had historically laid golden eggs for the family, was Dobach Mechanical Contracting. The company did about $55 million in gross revenue in 2013, about the same as in the peak prerecession year of 2006, and employed between two hundred and three hundred people, depending on seasonal needs. The company's 2014 revenue was expected to be flat. Its gross assets were worth about $12 million, but since the recession began, the company had taken on quite a bit of debt. Liabilities totaled about $7 million, and the company's book value had shrunk to about $5 million.

Debt was up sharply for two reasons. First, the company's gross revenue had fallen dramatically, and reluctant to let people go and make the hard decisions necessitated by the Great Recession, the company took on debt to keep those people working even while sustaining operating losses. Second, Generations Real Estate LLC, the newest of the family's business entities, had at Casey's urging invested in a real estate partnership in South Florida in 2005. What at first looked like a slam dunk quickly turned into a debacle due to the complete decimation of the beachfront high-rise business. Due to several massive capital calls, the family had to utilize Dobach Mechanical funds to prop up some of Generations Real Estate's debt.

The older real estate operation, Dobach Family Real Estate Inc. was started by Leon and owned the company's main building, warehouses, and a couple of smaller office/industrial buildings. The gross value of that entity was about $15 million, with about $4 million of debt. Dobach Family Real Estate was the source of Myra's income: 67 percent of the entity was owned in a trust for her benefit until she passed, at which time Fred, Velma, and Casey would inherit her interest in equal portions.

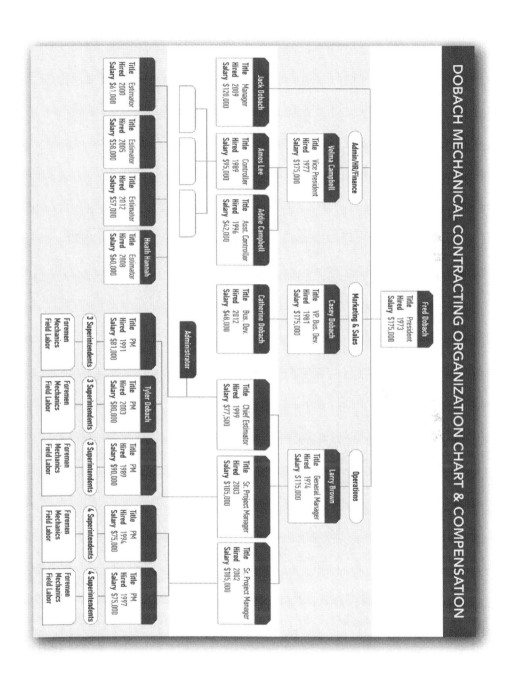

DOBACH MECHANICAL CONTRACTING ORGANIZATION CHART & COMPENSATION

Fred Dobach
Title President
Hired 1973
Salary $175,000

Admin/HR/Finance

Velma Campbell
Title Vice President
Hired 1977
Salary $175,000

Jack Dobach
Title Manager
Hired 2009
Salary $121,000

Amos Lee
Title Controller
Hired 1989
Salary $95,000

Addie Campbell
Title Asst. Controller
Hired 1996
Salary $62,000

Title Estimator
Hired 2000
Salary $61,000

Title Estimator
Hired 2005
Salary $58,000

Title Estimator
Hired 2012
Salary $57,000

Heath Hannah
Title Estimator
Hired 2008
Salary $60,000

Marketing & Sales

Casey Dobach
Title VP, Bus. Dev.
Hired 1981
Salary $175,000

Catherine Dobach
Title Bus. Dev.
Hired 2012
Salary $60,000

Administrator

Tyler Dobach
Title PM
Hired 1991
Salary $81,000

Title PM
Hired 2003
Salary $80,000

Title PM
Hired 1989
Salary $90,000

3 Superintendents

Foremen
Mechanics
Field Labor

3 Superintendents

Foremen
Mechanics
Field Labor

3 Superintendents

Foremen
Mechanics
Field Labor

Operations

Larry Brown
Title General Manager
Hired 1974
Salary $115,000

Title Chief Estimator
Hired 1999
Salary $77,500

Title Sr. Project Manager
Hired 2003
Salary $105,000

Title Sr. Project Manager
Hired 2002
Salary $105,000

Title PM
Hired 1994
Salary $75,000

Title PM
Hired 1997
Salary $75,000

4 Superintendents

Foremen
Mechanics
Field Labor

4 Superintendents

Foremen
Mechanics
Field Labor

17

STOCK OWNERSHIP

Dobach Mechanical Contracting Inc. (S)
Origin 1955

Gross Value	$12,000,000
Debt & Liabilities	$7,000,000
Net Worth	**$5,000,000**

Owner	Value	% Owned
Myra	$0	0.0%
Fred	$1,500,000	30.0%
Velma	$1,500,000	30.0%
Casey	$1,500,000	30.0%
Jack	$125,000	2.5%
Tyler	$125,000	2.5%
Addie	$125,000	2.5%
Cathrine	$125,000	2.5%
	$5,000,000	**100.0%**

Dobach Family Real Estate Inc. (S)
(company real estate, apartments)

Gross Value	$15,000,000
Debt & Liabilities	$4,000,000
Net Worth	**$11,000,000**

Owner	Value	% Owned
Myra	$7,370,000	(trust) 67.0%
Fred	$1,210,000	11.0%
Velma	$1,210,000	11.0%
Casey	$1,210,000	11.0%
	$11,000,000	100%

Generations Real Estate (LLC)
(residential development, commercial, retail, and multifamily spec ownership)

Gross Value	$12,000,000
Debt & Liabilities	$12,000,000
Net Worth	**$0**

Owner	Value	% Owned
Fred, Manager	$0	1.0%
Daphne	$0	1.0%
Jack	$0	15.5%
Tyler	$0	15.5%
Velma, Manager	$0	1.0%
Arthur	$0	1.0%
Addie	$0	31.0%
Casey, Manager	$0	1.0%
Miller	$0	1.0%
Libbie	$0	10.6%
Lisa	$0	10.6%
Catherine	$0	10.6%
	$0	**100.0%**

That was a quick snapshot of the family, the key employees, and the various business entities. Now, back to our challenges...

///
Early March 2014

The hastily called family meeting was a little unsettling in that most knew little or nothing about why we were convening. It was also awkward in the sense that family from both generations were sitting in. Normally, G2 had meetings just among themselves; now G3 and key managers were suddenly pulled in. There was an uneasy foreboding in the air as we started.

"Thanks for coming everyone," Fred said nervously. His expression was even more dour than usual as he looked around the large conference table. "Where's Tyler? I swear, that boy is never on time!"

"I told him about the meeting along with everybody else," said Velma. "He knew we were getting together this afternoon."

"Who knows what he has gotten himself into? Well, let's go ahead and get started. If Tyler comes in, we'll just try and catch him up."

Fred, Velma, and Casey proceeded to relate to Jack, Addie, Heath, Catherine, Larry, and Amos all they had discussed with Barney Smith of First National that morning. Following that lengthy exposition, Fred looked around the table and said, "So that's our situation. What questions have you all got...and do you have any recommendations?"

Amos said huffily, "I don't know what Barney's talking about. Not that much has changed in my view."

"Damn right! I'd like to box his ears and get another bank in here so we can kick those sons of bitches right out!" muttered Casey.

Jack added, "Maybe that's not the way I would have phrased it, but that does need to be among our very first steps. If First National does pull our line of credit, it could make things awfully tough in the short run and could potentially be catastrophic. We need to make sure that if it's not First National, we at least have a credit facility somewhere."

"That seems like a good idea," said Velma. "Why don't you and Addie work on identifying two or three alternative credit sources and get back to us with recommendations?"

"Will do," said Jack, looking at Addie, who averted her eyes and fumbled nervously with her pen. "Amos, I'm sure we're going to need your help on this as well."

"Of course," replied Amos. "But you have to remember, I have about a thousand other things on my plate right now. Tax season is—"

"What are we going to do about Generations Real Estate?" Velma interrupted. "The bank was pretty pointed about making sure we don't have any more money leaving the family's core business to prop up Generations. If we didn't have that thing hanging, we might not be having this conversation at all."

"There's not one thing wrong with Generations Real Estate!" thundered Casey. "My general partner assures me that everything is in order down there; there won't be any more capital calls, and it's going to be a home run for us. Just give it a few more years—you'll see!"

"We might not have a few more years, Uncle Casey," said Jack. "The issue isn't whether it's going to be a good long-term investment; it probably will be. The issue is what Florida real estate in general and Generations specifically are likely to do in the next ninety days to eighteen months."

"You don't know squat about this, Jack," Casey asserted. "I know you've got that fancy education and everything, but you haven't been in business long enough to know that in a situation like this you have to be patient and wait things out."

"With all due respect, Casey, it might be kind of hard to wait this one out if the bank pulls our operating line. If our working capital declines and the bonding company moves to take over our jobs, it would be a nightmare for us."

Fred interjected heatedly, "If you spent more time with our books instead of buying rounds of drinks at the nineteenth hole—"

"Screw you, Fred!" Casey shot back with blood in his eye. The two glared at each other.

"All right, all right, boys!" Velma said, "We have a problem to solve here, and the two of you need to focus! We need to plan for what we're going to do, and hoping it will get better with time isn't going to satisfy First National."

"What's this business Barney was talking about with these odd payments going out to vendors no one has ever heard of?" asked Fred.

"He doesn't know what he's talking about," Addie stammered. "Everybody knows our approval process; nothing gets through unless it is one hundred percent legit. Everybody knows that."

"That's right," Amos echoed.

"Well," said Fred, "we still need to look into it and respond to the bank's concerns. We can't just ignore it and pretend like they haven't raised the issue. Jack, I want you to get with Amos and Addie, and dig in a little bit to see what you can find."

"I don't need anyone, Jack included, looking over my shoulder!" Addie exclaimed. "I'll take care this; if there are any problems, I'll let you know."

"Addie, there is no reason to be defensive," Velma stated sooth-ingly. "Jack would just be like having a fresh set of eyes looking at things. A different perspective might be a good thing."

"I don't want anybody poking around in my department!" Addie shouted shrilly. "No one else ought to be messing around getting in my way and screwing up my routines! If there's anything to be found in this stupid charge, I'll find it."

"OK, honey," Velma replied meekly, her face registering surprise at the intensity of Addie's outburst. Addie was usually so quiet...

"I don't see how it could hurt to have Jack look into it. By god, for all the money he's earning, we ought to try to get some value out of him and that pointy-headed education," Casey commented.

"Thanks for the vote of confidence, Uncle Casey," Jack said.

"All right, I think we have a plan," Fred said. "I'm reluctant to get all worked up over this; after all, it's not like we don't have plenty of other things to do around here. But we need to have something we can present to the bank. Amos, you're going to have to do some research and figure out how to put together a business plan the bank will like. Jack and Addie, you're going to look into this foolish-ness about odd checks going out to unknown vendors, plus talk to First National's competitors. And Casey, you need to get with your partners on that real estate deal and get some kind of specific finan-cial projections for where things stand. We can't afford another cap-ital call. Make sure their projections match up with their big talk."

"I think it's bullshit, but I'll do it," Casey grumbled.

"Let's all get back together in three weeks' time and see where we stand, OK?"

Catherine spoke up for the first time. "Uncle Fred, the bank wants to see a comprehensive business plan from us in ninety days, correct? Waiting three weeks until we get together again burns up almost one-fourth of our allotted time. Do you think we have the luxury of waiting that long?"

Jack gave Catherine a nod of encouragement.

"Don't worry your pretty little head, Catherine. We've been through ups and downs with the bank and the bonding company before. All this will pass in no time, you'll see," Fred reassured her.

Catherine looked down, her mouth tightly drawn.

"I'm with Catherine, Dad." Jack said. "I think we really need to get to work on this as quickly as we can and set an aggressive pace. It could be a critical time for us. We don't want to make the mistake of treating this threat too casually."

"Why don't you do that, Big Brain?" sneered Casey. "You don't have all that much to do around here and plenty of free time on your hands. Why don't you put all that MBA horsepower to work and come up with something brilliant?"

"Back off, Casey," Fred blurted. Pausing a bit and looking at Jack, he said, "Casey's being a blowhard as usual, but this might be a good assignment for you, son, given all your experience assessing companies, looking at numbers, and putting together *pro forma* financials. You might be the right guy to help Amos with this."

Jack smiled, "It'll be my pleasure, Dad."

Amos shot a questioning look at Fred but said nothing.

"All right, that settles things. We'll get back together in three weeks and see what everybody's found out then."

IV

Late March 2014

It was now late March, and we got together for our second all-hands meeting to discuss First National's unwelcome news and what we were going to do about shoring up our finances and producing our first formal business plan.

"Thanks for coming everybody," said Fred. "And thanks for blessing us with your presence this time, Tyler."

Tyler, unhappy about being called out, looked down at his hands, his eyes shifting nervously back and forth.

"And where's Addie? Can we not get perfect attendance for even one meeting?"

"She was here little while ago," Velma said. "Something really important must have come up."

"Maybe her cat has a hairball," Casey grumbled.

"That's enough out of you, Casey! You were a jerk in our last meeting, and I'm not going to have you bullying everybody this time! If you don't have anything nice to say, just keep your mouth shut!" Velma blurted.

"Sure, sis, I'll keep my trap shut—until I have something to say," Casey shot back.

"All right, all right! For god's sake, let's not get sidetracked with a bunch of foolishness between you two," Fred said wearily. "Let's figure out what kind of progress we've made. Casey, what did you hear from the Florida people?"

"I talked to them for quite a while," Casey related as he shared a stack of financial projections with the group. "Here's what they're showing the limited partners for the rest of 2014, as well as for the full years 2015 to 2016. Cash flows and profits look good, and as I told you, we shouldn't have any more trouble with capital calls. Generations Real Estate will stand on its own from this point forward, and the GP assures me that we'll have enough free cash flow in the next year or two to be able to make distributions. We can gradually pay back the money Dobach Mechanical and the family real estate company put in."

"How confident are you in those numbers, Uncle Casey?" Jack asked. "We've seen rosy projections from these guys before."

"I'm one hundred percent!" Casey said. "The guys in Florida have just as many letters behind their names as you do, Jack. We'll have no more trouble out of Generations."

Fred said, "That's a relief, Casey. We can't afford to put one more dollar into it, and we need to show the bank that Generations can start distributing money instead of consuming it. Jack, why don't you review those numbers to make sure they're realistic and maybe back them off a little bit? We know the bank won't take the projections at face value; they're going to assume more conservative figures, and we need to see if less optimistic numbers will still help our case."

"Will do, Dad!" Jack said enthusiastically.

"Amos, how is it coming with your research on putting together a business plan?"

"Well," Amos said meekly, "I haven't made much progress. I've been pulling the corporate tax information together, plus doing the year-end numbers for the two real estate entities. And I have to have your individual tax returns done by April 15. Plus, we've been closing the books on March. I just haven't had much time to dig into an entirely new project."

"We understand, Amos," Fred said. "We know how much you have on your plate, and we appreciate all you do. But this is important, and as soon as you're done with the taxes, this needs to be your highest priority."

"OK, said Amos, "I'll get on it as soon as I can."

Catherine and Jack exchanged concerned looks. Larry shook his head and began making notes.

"Wow!" Tyler exclaimed. "I wish you guys were that patient with me when one of my projects gets sideways. You come down on me like a ton of bricks when I get off schedule, but I don't hear any pats on the back when I make a bunch of money for this company!" Looking directly at Fred, he said in a loud voice, "You treat Amos better than you treat your own son!"

Fred glared at his younger son but said nothing.

Velma said, "Tyler, you might have a good point there. We probably do need to give people more pats on the back when they do a good job. But that's a discussion we can have at another time. Right now we're focused on trying to get through this bank issue and avoiding the bonding company becoming involved."

Tyler stared at his reflection in the conference table.

"What about these checks to strange vendors?" Casey asked. "Been able to get your big brain into action and figure something out, Jack?"

"Well, I have, actually, and First National might have done us a service in pointing out these irregularities. I pulled together a report"—Jack got a stack of printed pages and distributed them around the table—"of unusual checks that seem to fall outside our normal approval procedure. For most of them, I can't find anything that matches up with the names on the checks among our approved vendors, on the Internet, or in the phone book. I don't know who these people are. Something looks pretty fishy, and while none of the individual checks is huge, over the past year they add up to over $65,000! This definitely bears more looking into."

Amos cleared his throat and sniffed, "I have no idea how these checks got through. Someone had to approve them, but it wasn't me giving the authorization!"

"Maybe not, Amos," Fred said. "But we need to figure out what's going on here. Plenty of my friends in business have had issues with money going missing over the years. We wouldn't be the first family business to get ripped off. We need to figure this out—and pronto."

"I'll look into it," Amos said flatly.

"Amos," Velma said, "don't you have a bit of a conflict here? You're supposed to be approving all the checks that go out, and suddenly we find ones that are slipping through your foolproof system? I think Jack needs to continue to look into it, and we probably need to pull in someone from our accounting firm as well."

"That's an absurd waste of money!" Amos said. "I can handle this."

"I think Velma's suggestion is a good one," injected Catherine. Everyone looked at her in surprise; she rarely voiced her opinion so early in a meeting. "It only makes sense that we get somebody with one hundred percent objectivity looking into this. It could be pretty serious, and we need to get to the bottom of it."

Amos glared at Catherine.

"I'll tell you one other thing I think we ought to do," said Jack. "Angie and I were having dinner with Lisa and her husband, Allen. All of you know Allen, right? His family runs the gasoline business; they have all those Zippy Marts scattered around, and their revenue is more than triple ours. They've had their trouble with the real estate market, too, among other things. Allen's family hired this consultant when they had business and family trouble—Allen says they've had some real knockdown fights over the years—and they give him credit for turning their company around and helping them make improvements in the way they function as family. I think we ought to talk to their consultant; Allen raved about him. Catherine was there—what did you think?"

"I think when someone has a heart problem, they see a cardiologist. When someone has cancer, they see an oncologist. It seems to me that we have a pressing, time-constrained problem that we've never had to deal with before, and we may not be fully equipped with internal resources to handle it. Getting a specialist to help us diagnose the problem and develop a plan of action to pacify the bank makes a lot of sense," Catherine asserted in her matter-of-fact way.

The murmurings started immediately:

"What would something like this cost?"

"We've been burned by consultants in the past! Remember that guy Leon spent thousands with? He hated death, taxes, and consultants!"

"A consultant who worked with a convenience store chain isn't going to know beans about the mechanical contracting business!"

"It would take too long to train somebody to know all the nuances of our business!"

"That's a stupid idea; we already have a great CPA and a great attorney!"

"Jack asked me for my point of view," Catherine said, "and I gave it."

She fell silent. Heath looked at her sympathetically.

"Everyone, I know we haven't always had good luck with consultants in the past," Jack stated. "But I reviewed some of the work in those three-ring binders on the shelf there"—everyone looked at two massive binders—"and there is some really savvy information there. I think one of the reasons we felt like Granddad wasted money on those consultants was because we didn't do our part to implement their recommendations. You like to tell stories about his favorite saying 'death and taxes,' but I don't think he genuinely understood the other business constant: *change*. Besides, big businesses use consultants successfully all the time. I don't see how it would hurt us to at least talk to someone who specializes in family business situations like this."

Just then Velma's phone rang. It was Dr. Michaels, Addie's on-again, off-again psychiatrist. He said, "Velma, you need to come to the hospital."

"What's wrong, Dr. Michaels? Is something wrong with Addie?"

"Addie is in the emergency room, Velma. We don't know exactly what's wrong, but it looks like she's taken an overdose of sleeping pills. The ER doctor thinks she may have tried to take her own life."

Velma sprang from her chair and sprinted for the door. "I'll be right there!" she shouted as she dropped her phone.

"Wait! Velma! What's wrong? Let me drive you!" Casey shouted as he took off in pursuit.

V

Late March 2014

Dr. Michaels's call had riveted the family's attention on Addie, her parents, and her children. Our business issues were pressing, but this was a time for the family to close ranks.

The scene in the emergency room was chaotic. Doctors, nurses, and staffers were hustling and bustling about, patients and their families were coming in and out in varying degrees of distress, and ER attendants were shuffling papers, getting signatures, and entering information into computers. Everybody was moving at super speed; this part of the hospital seemed more like a busy airport than a place for healing.

Dr. Michaels was sitting with Velma and Casey when Arthur came in. They were waiting for a report from the emergency room physician, and Dr. Michaels was quizzing Velma on what turn of events had led up to Addie's attempted suicide.

"Have there been any big changes in Addie's life recently?" Dr. Michaels asked.

Velma replied, "Not really. You know that she's been down and lethargic for some time. She worries about her weight, wishes she could quit smoking, and constantly feels like a failure as a mother. All this is ground you've covered with her in the past, right?"

Dr. Michaels nodded.

"I mean, we've had some issues at work, but it's not like we haven't had challenges before. I can't imagine what would've led Addie to try something stupid like this."

"Neither can I," Arthur spoke for the first time. He'd never been a fan of Dr. Michaels and regarded psychiatrists more like witch doctors rather than fellow professionals. "It breaks my heart that my little girl is doing so poorly that she would try something like this. Could it be that it's not an overt attempt, Doctor? Maybe it was accidental."

"That's not what the ER docs think based on the amount she ingested," said Dr. Michaels gravely. "I wish we were able to explain it away that easily, Arthur, but it looks like this was a legitimate attempt by Addie to take her own life."

Arthur shuddered at the news. Tears streamed down Velma's face, and for once, Casey was silent and respectful.

Fred and Daphne came into the waiting area. "Is there anything at all we can do, Velma?" asked Daphne while giving her a warm embrace. "We feel so bad for Addie and for you. Anything at all?'"

"Thank you," said Velma. "Just you being here is plenty. I don't think there's anything any of us can do—except pray—until we hear from the doctor."

The family settled in uncomfortably, not knowing how long they'd have to wait. In a few minutes, the emergency room physician appeared and headed their way. Velma leaped to her feet. "What can you tell us, Doctor?"

The phone rang at Dobach Mechanical. Because none of the family members were in the office, it was routed to Larry Brown. "Morning, Ray," Larry said to the company's longtime surety agent. "Nice to hear from you, buddy; how's everything going?"

"Things are going well here," replied Ray. "But we've heard through the grapevine that not everything is going so well for you guys. What's going on?"

"Not too much," said Larry, wondering how bad news could possibly travel so fast. "We did have a little shot across the bow from the bank, and they want us to put together some reports and move some things around to make our financials look a little better, but you know how squirrelly banks are these days."

"Well, we do know they're awfully skittish right now, but I have to tell you, the bonding company gets very concerned when your bank is concerned." Ray continued. "It's only fair to let you know that we're going to have to keep a very close eye on things and raise the level of our monitoring of your projects and budgets going forward. I don't want to be all doom and gloom on you, Larry, but please pass this information on to Fred, Velma, and Casey soon as you can. We need to set up a meeting ASAP, and I'll be bringing my boss from the home office."

"Of course I will," Larry responded. "Thanks for the heads up." Larry hung up the phone and put his head into his gigantic hands. "I'm getting too old for this crap!" he mumbled to himself.

Jack was up to his elbows in paper with two laptops up and running on his desk when Catherine walked in. "Here, I brought you a cup of coffee," said Catherine.

"Thank you. I've already had half a dozen today; I guess one more won't hurt."

"This looks overwhelming," Catherine commented. "Have you been able to find anything?"

Jack replied, "Yes, I certainly have. The more I look into this business, the worse it appears. Somebody has been stealing. That's the only conclusion I can come up with. Worse, since access to company funds is tightly restricted, it has to be either a family member or Amos, who is practically like a family member. I'm afraid this isn't going to turn out well."

"Keep after it," Catherine encouraged. "This is important, and even though you'll probably uncover bad news, this is information we need to have."

There was a clatter in the hallway. Casey's wife, Amber, popped her head in the door. She was wearing the highest of high heels, tight jeans, and a bright pink V-neck sweater. "How y'all doin'? Y'all look so glum; did somebody's dog die?"

Jack and Catherine returned Amber's greeting without commenting on her ill-framed question. "I just dropped in to see if my sweetie Casey could run an errand with me, but he's not in his office. Do y'all know where he is?"

"He took Velma to the hospital," Catherine replied. "I guess you haven't heard about Addie. She may have attempted suicide. They're in the emergency room now waiting for news."

"Oh no!" Amber shrieked. "I'll get myself down there right away!" She scurried out the door.

Jack looked at Catherine. "Is it just me, or did it look like Amber's sweater was quite a bit more filled out than usual?"

"I noticed it, too," Catherine said smiling. "How could I not?"

"Oh crap! That reminds me of something," exclaimed Jack. He tapped on his computer and pulled up a digital copy of a check in the amount of $5,800 made out to Plastic Surgery Associates. "I was wondering how we could've rationalized a check made out to a plastic surgery firm. I know this is only circumstantial, but we may have just found who's been funneling company money for his personal use. This is going to require some explanation, I think. How do I present this to G2? Your dad might wring my neck! And what will Dad and Aunt Velma say?"

"Oh my!" Catherine exclaimed with a crestfallen expression. "I can't believe Dad would do anything like that. There has got to be a rational explanation! This is awful!"

In the emergency room, the attending physician was updating everyone. "Addie attempted to take her own life by ingesting an overdose of prescription sleeping pills. Presently she is stable, but she's not out of the woods yet. She's still unconscious, and her vital signs are depressed but within the normal range. We're going to have to admit her and place her in intensive care until she regains consciousness." As Velma wept silently, the doctor continued. "Who has Addie's healthcare power of attorney? We might need to make some medical decisions in the next few hours or days."

"I do," declared Arthur.

"Good, let me confer with you and Mrs. Campbell in more detail. It might be best for the rest of you to go home and wait for more news. It could be some time before Addie comes around."

Amber burst into the emergency room, ran up to Casey, and flung her arms around him. "Oh, honey bear, I'm so sorry! What can I do?"

Casey hugged his wife. "Hi, sweetie. Thanks for coming. Addie might be in a bad way, so we're just going to have to wait and see how things turn out."

Amber excitedly greeted the other family members who, as usual, gave her a civil but chilly reception.

"OK, everyone," said Arthur authoritatively. "Why don't you all clear out, and we'll keep you updated as we learn more. No point in all of us being here. Velma and I will stay with Addie while she gets admitted." Everyone exchanged hugs. Fred, Daphne, Casey, and Amber shuffled out the door to the parking area.

Once they were gone, Velma said to Arthur, "Why did she have to come? Things are bad enough without her sticking her nose into places where it doesn't belong. And it looks like this isn't her first visit to the hospital recently. That trashy sweater didn't leave much to the imagination."

Arthur patted Velma's hand and remained silent.

Fred wearily returned to the office. The flashing light on his telephone indicated he had voice mail. "Come see me soon as you get back," Larry's deep, gravelly voice echoed through the speaker. Larry rarely reached out to Fred or anyone else in the company. He was the most self-sufficient man Fred had ever known. "What now?" Fred murmured under his breath.

He walked down the hall and around the corner to Larry's office. "What's going on, Larry?" he asked.

"More unwelcome news, I'm afraid. The bonding company called, and they want a meeting ASAP. They are concerned about where we stand with the bank and how it could affect our bonded projects. Ray was pretty nice in the call, but it was obvious that they will be increasing their scrutiny. They could make things hard on us if they choose to."

"Jesus H. Christ!" exclaimed Fred, wishing he could light up. Why had he agreed to that stupid no-smoking policy? A drink would have been welcome, too. "What else can go wrong today? I thought at this stage in our careers, Larry, we'd be on cruise control, enjoying life and counting up our winnings. But this is been one of the worst periods I can remember. It just sucks all the enjoyment out of life to have to put up with crap like this!"

"Tell me about it," Larry agreed. "The prospect of retirement looks better all the time, doesn't it?"

"Hold on a minute there, buddy!" Fred said with a distraught look. "We need you now more than ever!"

"I know, I know. I'm just kidding. I'm not going anywhere. We'll find a way to get through this, Fred."

Jack walked into Larry's office. "I'm glad you guys are here. Allen Eastman called me. The consultant they use, Tom Hartwell, is in town. I told Allen we have an interest in speaking with him. If it's OK with you guys, I'll coordinate a meeting."

"I think it's a good idea," said Larry. "Given all that's going on right now, we might need somebody to help us get a handle on things."

"I'm not quite as excited as you two are about this guy," said Fred. "But if he is already in town I guess there's no harm in having him come over to visit. Want to tell him to come over first thing in the morning before we get too busy, say about seven thirty?"

"OK, will do, Dad. I'll give everyone a heads up," said Jack. With that he turned on his heel and departed.

"This guy could be a big help to us potentially, Fred," Larry pointed out.

"Maybe so. We'll see. Like I said, no harm in talking to the guy. I can't take any more bad news today; I'm going home. See you tomorrow, Larry."

"I'll say a prayer for Addie," Larry said as Fred exited.

VI

April 2014

We were getting together to meet with a family business consultant named Tom Hartwell. He came highly recommended from Allen Eastman's family and had been a big help to their convenience store business. That said, there was a good bit of skepticism and nervousness; we didn't know what to expect from the guy or how he might be able to help. And some family members still had a bad taste in their mouths due to Leon's poor experience with a consultant years ago.

Just before 7:30 a.m., people started filing into the conference room carrying their coffee, tablets, laptops, notepads, and pens. From the family there was Fred, Casey, Jack, Tyler, Heath, and Catherine. Larry and Amos were sitting in, too. Velma was at the hospital, having barely left Addie's bedside. At 7:25 a.m., our receptionist announced that Tom Hartwell had arrived.

As he entered the room, we sized him up. He was of average height and appeared to be in pretty good shape. He looked about fifty years old, had graying hair, and was dressed in a preppy outfit of khaki trousers, loafers, a white button-down shirt, and a navy blazer. He looked like a competent enough fellow but not necessarily one who could single-handedly turn around a troubled family or business, much less the kind of wizard capable of the things Allen's family ascribed to him. He carried only a small binder; he had no laptop, no stack of business cards, and no elaborate brochures. It didn't look like he was prepared for much of a razzle-dazzle presentation.

Fred kicked off the meeting. "Tom, thanks for visiting with us this morning. Why don't you tell us a little about yourself and what you do?"

"I'd be happy to, Fred," Tom replied. "First, let me say that I am very sorry to hear about Addie. I know that has to be uppermost in your minds right now; the needs of the family always outweigh the needs of the business. Having said that, I'm happy to answer any questions you have about me or my experience." Tom rattled off his academic qualifications, including an MBA from a prestigious school, his experience in the big-business world, how he'd come to run several businesses for other families, and some of the notable family companies he'd consulted for in the mechanical contracting industry. Tom continued. "I also know that you've been getting a little static from your bank and bonding company, and those have to be things that concern you, too."

Casey exclaimed, "It sounds like Allen may have been running his mouth! Nobody outside this room knows about those things! Where did you get that information?"

"You can't blame Allen," Tom replied evenly. "Most family businesses think they have secrets, but the reality is, there aren't very many secrets. In your business, everyone knows everyone else, and it's a very small world. News gets around the grapevine pretty quickly. As I mentioned, we have some other clients in mechanical and other types of construction, and we keep our ears pretty close to the ground."

Casey grumbled, "I still think I might need to take my son-in-law out behind the woodshed."

Fred interjected, "You're right, Tom, we have had a little notice from the bank and bonding company, but we're on top of that, and Amos is leading the charge to pull together our business plan and projected financials to get them squared away. Isn't that right, Amos?"

Amos looked generally in his boss's direction but didn't squarely meet Fred's gaze. "Well, I'm working on it, but I haven't made much progress so far. I told you about all the corporate and personal tax work, and there's a lot on my plate right now. But I'm going to make this a priority!"

Jack and Catherine exchanged glances, and Casey rolled his eyes.

Tom went on. "That's fine. I'm sure you are taking all necessary action—how could you not? If you don't mind me being very blunt, the question is: would you be better off hiring a subcontractor to help accelerate this project and get you into shape to meet the bank's expectations, or do you have the internal resources to do it and meet the deadline?"

Larry said, "That's a great analogy, Tom. In the old days, general contractors did everything: mechanical, plumbing, electrical, etc. Gradually, they realized that hiring specialists like us could accelerate their schedules, save money, and raise project quality. That's what you're proposing, right? You're basically a subcontractor with a specialized way of thinking and a particular skill set, correct?"

"That's right, Larry. This is what we do every day. I know you feel somewhat adrift and even disoriented due to Addie's situation and the bad news from the bank and bonding company. Here is something we've developed over the years that might help you understand what you're going through and put you more at ease."

Tom handed out copies of a diagram.

"We call this the *Change Model*. It was developed first by the late Virginia Satir and has been revised and extended by her protégé Jean McClendon. The model graphically represents the emotional stages of people or groups undergoing change and very much applies to families in business together. It is helpful for people who are changing, growing, shrinking, or dealing with unexpected internal or external forces. And virtually everyone is going through some form of personal, family, or work changes—some big, some small—at all times."

Everyone looked at the graphic Tom had passed around.

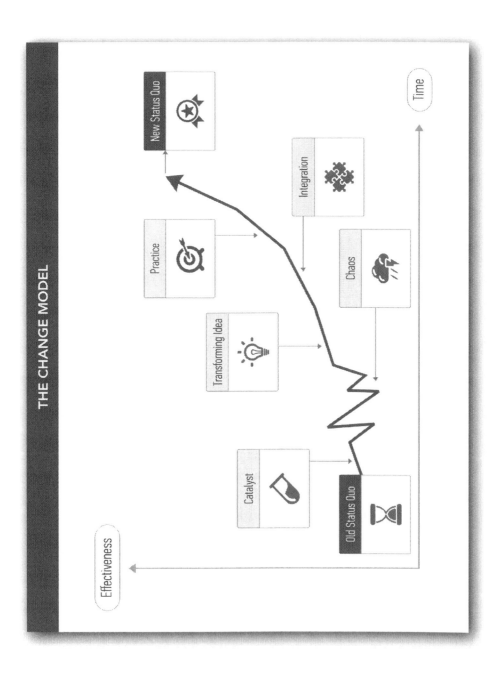

"The x-axis represents time; the y-axis is effectiveness. The first stage is *Status Quo*. Status Quo is benign, the normal, the familiar. Every day is more or less like the day before, and your routines are well established and predictable. Things are going reasonably smoothly, and they are comfortable. You've all heard of being in your comfort zone, correct?" Everyone nodded. "When it feels like the business is running on cruise control and there is reasonable harmony in the family, that's Status Quo."

"We all know what status quo means, Tom," Fred said pointedly.

Tom continued. "In the next stage, there is a *Catalyst*, often a foreign element interjected into your comfortable routines. In this case, it might be the meeting with the bank, or your family crisis. The Catalyst or the foreign element creates a new awareness that maybe things aren't so rosy or comfortable after all and that changes, maybe big ones, are on the horizon. You might feel suddenly like the rug has been snatched from beneath your feet."

Lots of affirmative nods indicated agreement with the analogy.

"That brings you to the next stage: *Chaos*. In Chaos, you are suddenly on unfamiliar ground. Things aren't as predictable as they were, and the usual routines and ways of doing business that you've come to rely on are no longer producing satisfactory results. For example, many contractors haven't been able to generate the margins they used to before the Great Recession utilizing the same business practices they'd traditionally used. For you in particular, the bank has required that you produce a business plan in a very short time frame, but they've not given you much track to run on in terms of what it is supposed to look like or why the plan is supposed to give them the reassurance they want. Since you don't exactly know how to go about this, not having done this before as a business or family, this has put a new, unfamiliar challenge in your path. And not knowing precisely the consequences of failing to meet the bank's request creates uncertainty and fear. All that contributes to Chaos.

There may be lots of ways to meet the challenges of Chaos. For example, you've asked Amos to get on the development of a business plan, but Amos already has plenty of other things to do, and he may be a little unsure about where to start. And if the bank and bonding company aren't reassured, then another, bigger Chaos element will be dumped into your lap. And Addie's situation in addition to the business challenges is making things even more chaotic."

"I'm sure I can handle this business plan thing, Tom," Amos asserted coolly.

"I'm confident you folks can do this," Tom said. "But the fact is that the bank's demand represents change, and you all are in a state of Chaos at the moment."

"I agree!" Jack and Catherine said almost simultaneously. There were a couple of nervous chuckles.

Tom continued. "During the period of Chaos, performance and effectiveness drop and become very uneven. You may feel miserable and hopeless. Some days you think you have things well in hand, and on other days you think you'll never get through this unsettled period. Your mind is consumed with the changes and possible ripple effects. Your imagination goes into overdrive, and you're assaulted with negative mental pictures.

"Chaos can go on for quite a long time, or it could be over pretty abruptly. The natural reaction during Chaos is to retreat to the old, the known, and the familiar: in other words, to the old Status Quo. However, that's self-defeating behavior. In this case you know the bank won't allow you to not conform to their wishes. That's a legitimate threat to your business, and you're going to have to develop the required plans to their satisfaction or face serious business—and family—consequences."

"How do we get out of Chaos?" asked Larry, intently looking at Tom's graphic.

"Emerging from Chaos successfully depends on the next stage which is the *Transforming Idea*. While in Chaos, you are inclined to try lots of solutions that you may not have tried to apply before. For example, you're talking to me about helping out with this project. One or more of the many things that you try during the period of Chaos will take hold and bear fruit. The Transforming Idea—and there could be more than just one—is your path out of Chaos. It gives you hope and a track to run on so you can begin to dig your way out. In a sense, Chaos is good in that all of the anxiety and stress you're undergoing requires you to roll up your sleeves and work hard to search for that Transforming Idea. Does all this make sense to you all? Is it resonating at all?"

Several heads nodded.

"The Transforming Idea leads you to *Integration*. During the Integration stage, you begin to get a sense that you're getting a handle on things, and optimism as well as effectiveness increases. But a warning about this stage: it's easy to overreact to minor setbacks. Your optimism has soared, and you see light at the end of the tunnel, but with any little setback, you fear you may be facing an entirely new element of Chaos. You have to be on your guard in this stage not to overreact to small setbacks. For example, we might produce a business plan that the bank accepts and make changes accordingly only to have the bonding company come swiftly around raising a new set of issues. In fact, we should be proactive and go ahead and anticipate that this will be the case so we can get ahead of the curve."

Larry said, "That seems wise. There's always another shoe to drop."

"After that comes *Practice*. You have learned new things, new skills, and now you're practicing new behaviors. At this point, the Transforming Idea is yours. You again have a handle on things and are gradually easing back into what's normal for you; in other words, you're headed for a *New Status Quo* where effectiveness has increased, and you have established a new higher-level normal."

"This is all great, Tom," Casey said acerbically. "But it looks like a bunch of academic mumbo-jumbo to me. Why are you emphasizing this so much?"

"Great question, Casey," Tom replied. "Managing change is hard, and most family businesses grossly underestimate the difficulty they'll have during periods of rapid or unexpected change. Here, you have the family side of things to deal with as well as the business side. Your attention at the moment is focused on the bank's short-term demand, but there's another big, once-a-generation change looming. You, Velma, Fred, Larry, and Amos are all nearing retirement ages in the next few years. That means the next generation—Tyler, Catherine, Heath, Addie, and Jack—are preparing to face plenty of changes, too. During the process of intergenerational transition for a family business—and this has nothing to do with the bank's demand or Addie's situation right now—there are about a million things that need to be explicitly addressed to assure the intergenerational handoff goes smoothly. For example, look at this list of things that all have to be done— pretty much simultaneously—for a business to run well. Someone has to be responsible for each and every one of them, and that means a steep learning and preparation curve for G3."

Tom passed out another paper. Fred, daunted by the list, clapped his hand to his head.

"I don't know how far along you are in your intergenerational succession discussions, but that transition is going to happen in the next few years, and that is a massive change that, in my experience, most family businesses don't handle very well. My point, Casey and everyone else, is that the Change Model may help you understand the anxiety and stress you're going through now, as well as prepare you for other changes you can and should anticipate. It's a tool we can refer back to over and over so we can attempt to assess where you are along the scale and take appropriate action for getting you into a better place. And if you can anticipate the predictable changes like intergenerational succession, you can plan and get ahead so the disruptions aren't so drastic."

THE DEPTH OF WHAT IS REQUIRED TO HAVE A SUCCESSFUL BUSINESS

Areas of Management Attention and Expertise

FINANCIAL		OPERATIONAL		ORGANIZATIONAL	
• A/R Management	• Discounts	• Bid Tracking	• Material Tracking	• Accountability	• Job Definition
• Accrual Accounting	• Distribution of Profit	• Bidding	• Office Procedures	• Assigning Authority	• Leadership
• Balance Sheet, Income & Cash Flow	• Financial Comparisons	• Computer Estimating Software	• OSHA Regulations	• Assigning Responsibility	• Meetings
• Banking	• Financial Ratios	• Contract Management	• Policies and Procedures	• Benefit Programs	• Mission & Values
• Billings	• Financial Software	• Engineering	• Project Management	• Board of Directors	• Monitoring
• Bonding	• Gross Margins	• Equipment Maintenance	• Purchasing	• Chain of Command	• Performance
• Book vs. Tax Accounting	• Insurance	• Equipment Use & Costs	• Quality Assurance	• Change Management	• Orientation
• Bookkeeping	• Interpreting Financial Statements	• Estimating	• Resource Allocation	• Communication	• Motivation
• Break Even	• Lease and Purchasing Decisions	• Finding Work	• Safety	• Drug Testing	• Partnerships
• Budgeting	• Lien Laws	• Getting Paid for Work	• Scheduling	• Employee Policies	• Performance Review
• Cash Controls	• Overhead Allocations	• Inventory Control	• Selling Work	• Employment Laws	• Performance Standards
• Cash Forecasting	• Payroll Laws and Rules	• Job Costing	• Shipping & Receiving	• Exit Strategies	• Personal Effectiveness
• Cash Management	• Payroll Taxes	• Labor Burden	• Tool Controls	• Goal Setting	• Personality Profiles
• Chart of Accounts	• Percentage of Completion	• Labor Tracking	• Training Programs	• Health Insurance	• Prioritization
• Completed Project Basis	• S-Corp Versus C-Corp	• Loaded Labor Rates	• Vehicle Controls	• Hiring/Firing	• Recruiting
• Corporate Compliance	• Warranty Accruals	• Logistics	• Vehicle Maintenance	• Identify Critical	• Reporting
• CPAs	• Workers Compensation	• Managing	• Warehouse Organization	Success Factors	• Sales Management
• Credit Policies		• Material Specs & Costs		• Incentive Programs	• Strategy
• Depreciation		Subcontractors			• Team Building

"I like it," Jack asserted. "I think you've hit the nail on the head. I've never seen this before, but I believe it accurately represents the continuum that we as a family business are on both right now and in the coming years. I think it's a handy tool."

Tom remained silent and gazed around the table. Casey had his massive forearms folded across his belly and was leaning back in his chair with an impassive expression. Catherine, Tyler, and Jack had taken extensive notes and were fully engaged. Amos was doodling on his pad, having taken just a couple of notes. Fred leaned forward in his chair indicating that he was listening intently. Larry had made about a page and a half of notes and was continuing to write furiously.

The visitor spoke up. "I have one other handout. We call this our magic bullet for helping family businesses enjoy maximum harmony while also having a healthy business. It's a family-business-oriented ten-step business planning model."

He passed the papers out, and all looked at their handouts.

"You can see how this is a closed-loop planning process, and we've developed and modified it over the years so that it produces predictably outstanding results. I don't know yet, just having met you this morning, but I would suspect that this process will produce exactly what the bank is looking for. The good news is that, while it would pacify both bank and bonding, it would also produce additional long-term results for you in both the family and the business. It's not just a compliance exercise; this is a tool for helping all of you get more out of life and more out of your business."

"It looks overly complicated to me," Amos said.

"It might look complicated at first glance," Tom replied evenly, "but it's pretty simple in practice. After all, it's only ten steps. And a surprising by-product of this business planning process is that by increasing the amount of communication and sharing you do as a business, family harmony and satisfaction tend to go up, too!"

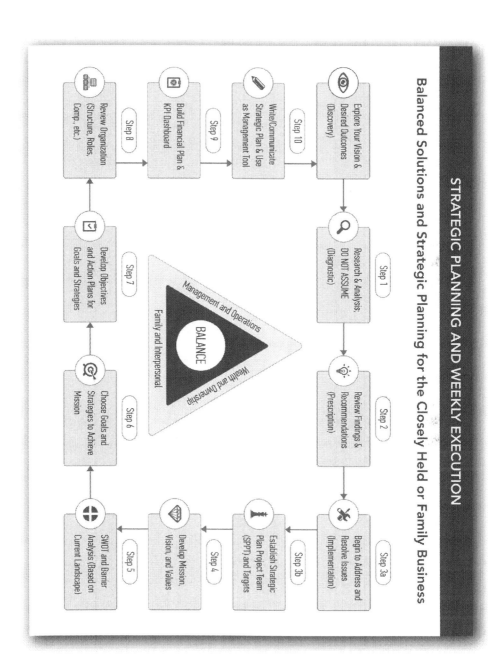

STRATEGIC PLANNING AND WEEKLY EXECUTION

Balanced Solutions and Strategic Planning for the Closely Held or Family Business

Step 1 — Research & Analysis. DO NOT ASSUME (Diagnostic)

Step 2 — Review Findings & Recommendations (Prescription)

Step 3a — Begin to Address and Resolve Issues (Implementation)

Step 3b — Establish Strategic Plan Project Team (SPPT) and Targets

Step 4 — Develop Mission, Vision, and Values

Step 5 — SWOT and Barrier Analysis (Based on Current Landscape)

Step 6 — Choose Goals and Strategies to Achieve Mission

Step 7 — Develop Objectives and Action Plans for Goals and Strategies

Step 8 — Review Organization (Structure, Roles, Comp., etc.)

Step 9 — Build Financial Plan & KPI Dashboard

Step 10 — Write/Communicate Strategic Plan & Use as Management Tool

Explore Your Vision & Desired Outcomes (Discovery)

BALANCE — Management and Operations / Family and Interpersonal / Wealth and Ownership

"What's this triangle diagram in the middle of the model?" asked Catherine.

"Great question," Tom replied. "This is our Balanced Triangle Model for working with family businesses. Let me give you a quick introduction. The family is always the base of the triangle, the most important part. The left-hand side represents the management and operations of your business, and the right side represents wealth, money, and power in the family and business systems. It's our belief that all three sides of the triangle ought to be in balance for a business family to enjoy optimal health. However, the reality is that most people in family businesses spend about ninety-five percent of their time on the left-hand side. They devote inordinate amounts of time and energy to the operations of the business and try to fit the other two elements into their spare time—of which there is none. Our work, therefore, is to try to create a healthy equilateral triangle that is defined by the fourth dimension you see there: BALANCE."

"I like this!" Jack exclaimed. "This balance model makes a lot of sense to me; it really resonates. How would you say we stack up in terms of balance, Tom?"

"Well—" Tom chewed on his lip while he pondered his response. "Let's say I've seen other family-owned businesses with a lot less balance than yours." The group had a chuckle at their own expense. "But you shouldn't feel bad. A family business is a stern mistress, and yours commanded an inordinate amount of time, attention, and love from its founder Leon. Fred, Velma, and Casey learned their business and management habits from their father, so they have really never seen an example of a holistic, balanced approach to running a business and family. That's one of the reasons I'm here now. You're doing business planning as a result of a mandate from your bank, but maybe you're also getting a sense of other potential long-term payoffs—one of which is better family communication and health."

Fred looked at his watch. Surprisingly, the meeting had been going for about an hour and a half. "Well, Tom, you've given us a lot to think about here. We're going to need to put our heads together and, of course, get my sister Velma in the loop. We'll get back to you in a few weeks to see if you might be able to help us."

"Thanks, Fred," Tom said. "Here is my recommendation. You can take it or leave it. I know Velma can't be here this morning, but the rest of you certainly are. I recommend you take fifteen minutes immediately after I leave this room and discuss what we've shared, and then decide on your best course of action. My reasoning is this: when you leave this room, you are going to be besieged with meetings, phone calls, e-mails, and people needing answers from you. This meeting is going to fade from memory pretty quickly. While everyone is here and engaged, put your heads together and come up with a decision."

"Tom, that's just not how we do things around here!" Fred insisted as he slapped his palm on the table. "We like to make consensus decisions, and we like to be cautious. I always say, 'Don't get in a hurry to make a bad decision.'"

Tom paused and, with a look of intensity and gravity on his face, replied, "Fred, that's one of the reasons family businesses get themselves in trouble. They don't have well-developed processes for making difficult decisions, and that causes them to take too long or, worse, decide not to make any decision at all. I don't mean to be harsh or appear critical, but if what I've heard is true, you don't have the luxury of a few weeks to deliberate over how you are going to answer the bank's demand. Margaret Thatcher once said, 'Consensus is the absence of leadership.' This is an important inflection point for you, and I would be doing you a disservice if I didn't help you determine a specific course of action. I'm not trying to be pushy, but you need a push just now!"

"He's right, Dad," Jack said. "We need to get on this right away, and we don't have a few weeks."

"I hate to say it, but I think I'm in agreement with my egghead nephew," Casey growled.

"Hold on a minute, everybody!" Fred exclaimed. "Let's excuse Tom, and…OK, fine, we'll take his advice and meet for fifteen minutes. If we can come up with a decision in that time, we will. Otherwise, we'll go with our normal procedure and consider it a little longer. I'll set my watch for fifteen minutes, and we'll talk about where we go from here. Tom, thanks for coming this morning."

Fred rose from his chair, signaling that Tom's time was up.

"You're welcome," Tom said. He shook hands with everybody and exited the conference room.

Fred closed the door. There was a moment of tense, uncomfortable silence. Jack spoke up first. "I think Tom Hartwell is just what the doctor ordered! He's got extensive experience with family businesses, he's done strategic planning for others so he could answer the bank's demand efficiently and quickly, he has a well-developed planning process, and he's a known quantity in the sense that he is currently helping Allen's family business much to their satisfaction."

"I don't think we need any outsider to come in here and help us!" Amos spat. "Besides, at a time like this we hardly have the money to be throwing at expensive consultants!"

"Amos," Casey said, "it's good to be thrifty, but there is also such a thing as being penny wise and pound foolish. Nobody's more skeptical of consultants than me—I remember Dad's fiasco. But Tom impressed me as being a good man for getting us out of hot water with the bank at the very least, and maybe he has something to offer even beyond that. You said yourself you haven't made much progress; maybe Tom could jump-start us."

Amos looked down with lips tightly pursed.

Larry spoke up. "Folks, I've got about two and half pages of notes here, and that guy impressed the hell out of me. Just going back over these notes, I'm finding about ten things Tom talked about that we need to do and probably should've been doing years ago. If I have a vote, I'd say we need to get that guy on board yesterday!"

Everyone looked at Fred. "Wow!" he said. "I didn't know you all felt so strongly about it. Why don't we sleep on it and get back together early next week to talk a little bit more? Maybe Tom could help us—"

Larry spoke up again. "Fred, we started in this business together, and we've worked hand in glove for all these years, never having had a harsh word between us. But I'm saying right now that waiting to hire somebody like Tom would be a damn fool mistake. We're in the business of managing projects and schedules, and the bank has laid out a big project with a tight schedule and some potentially ugly consequences. I think we need this guy."

Catherine stated, "Uncle Fred, this is no different than, say, hiring a nutritionist to formulate a diet to help you lose fifteen pounds and have a healthier lifestyle. Tom can coach us and get us to a better place. Seems like this would be a prudent choice and a wise course of action."

"She's right, Fred; it's a no-brainer," Casey stated as a matter of fact.

"All right, all right," Fred said stonily. "Seems I'm being shouted down! Let's get this genius in here and see what he's made of. But I'm warning you: if he screws up or gets off schedule or makes things worse, I'm going to kick him right out the door!"

"That's not exactly a ringing endorsement, Dad, but it is the right decision to make," said Jack.

Catherine asked, "What about Aunt Velma? We need to get her in the loop."

Casey said, "I'll talk to her. I'm going by the hospital anyway. Velma needs a break; she's been with Addie almost from the first minute this thing happened."

Fred asked, "Who's going to call Tom Hartwell and let him know he has a new guinea pig to play with?"

"I'll take care of that, Dad, if it's OK with you," Jack replied.

"Do it," instructed Fred.

As the meeting adjourned, Catherine informed Casey, "Please tell Aunt Velma that Lisa, Libbie, and I are going over to Addie's house to check on things, clean up, and feed her cats. I wouldn't want her to worry about little things like that."

"I'll take care of it, honey," replied Casey.

VII
April 2014

Libbie, Lisa, and Catherine arrived at Addie's home. She still lived in the same house she and her ex-husband had bought in the late 1990s. Her three children (ages seventeen, fourteen, and twelve), were able to sleep in the same bedrooms they had as youngsters when they visited. Addie didn't need as much space as she once did, but she hated change and preferred keeping to a familiar environment.

The three sisters proceeded up the driveway. Lisa, dressed as usual in brightly colored exercise clothing, spoke first. "This yard is in need of some serious TLC! I know Addie's not big on outdoor work or gardening, but these bushes are covering up her windows, and there are branches littering the ground everywhere! It almost looks like the place is uninhabited."

"It certainly doesn't look like it did when Stephen lived here," said Libbie. "He was always finding some outdoor project to work on; maybe he was trying to stay away from Addie." The sisters shared an uncomfortable giggle.

"That's mean!" Lisa exclaimed. "You're right, though; Addie can be a real downer when she wants to be. It's funny—when we were little and she babysat for us, I don't remember her being that way. She wasn't what you'd call energetic, but she was always very giving, played games with us, and generally was more like a caring aunt than a cousin."

Catherine produced a key and opened the back door. "Oh my god!" she exclaimed. "What's that smell?"

Lisa said, "Nobody has been emptying the cat's litter boxes, that's for sure!"

They held their noses, and coughed as they entered the house. The scene was shocking. Everyone knew Addie liked cats, but there were at least a half dozen that the siblings could see, and there may have been more hiding out in other parts of the house. The place reeked of cat urine and foul litter boxes. Adding to the mess were piles of dirty dishes stacked in every imaginable place, unemptied trash cans, newspapers and magazines strewn everywhere, and general clutter. There were overflowing ashtrays in every room, clothes and linens tossed liberally about the floor, and a vast number of opened and unopened UPS and FedEx boxes from every Internet merchant one could imagine.

"It's so dark in here,' Libbie said. "All the curtains are drawn. It's practically funereal."

"This would be a depressing place to live," Lisa opined. "I know Addie isn't the happiest person, but if we'd seen this, we would've had a warning sign that her dysfunction was greater than we suspected."

"You're right," Catherine said. "This looks like a genuine cry for help."

The young ladies busily opened doors and windows so the spring breeze could flush out the vile odors, and they searched the utility closet and under the kitchen sink for buckets, mops, sponges, and cleaning supplies. "This is a much bigger cleanup than we had anticipated," sighed Libbie. "Maybe we should just get the janitorial service that cleans up our office buildings to come over here and take care of it."

"First," Catherine pointed out, "I'm not sure that's a legitimate use for a company vendor. Second, we told Aunt Velma we would do it. Third, it is the least we can do for Addie considering how much she did for us when we were growing up."

"OK," Libbie said glumly. "But this is *not* what I signed up for!"

"Oh, Libbie, it'll be fun!" Lisa said. "Think of it like sculpting. Your goal is to try to find the beauty under all this mess. You're a gifted artist; you see the parallel, don't you?"

"Maybe," Libbie said. "Catherine, what's the latest on Addie?"

"Dad said there hasn't been much change. She is still unconscious, and the doctors don't know exactly when—or even if—she'll come around. Her vital signs are stable, they say, and they have some hope. All in all, there's not much new to report."

"I hope she gets better soon!" Lisa said brightly. "I don't know much about suicide. Where does one go after a failed attempt? Do things just go back to normal? Are we supposed to act as if nothing has happened the next time we see her? Maybe Dr. Michaels can coach us."

At Dobach Mechanical, Jack dialed his dad on the intercom. "Dad, I've been digging into the unexplained checks, and I've found something I think you need to see. Can you come into my office?"

"I'll be right down," said Fred.

After he closed the door behind Fred, Jack pulled up the digital image of the check he and Catherine had looked at the day before. "I'm not sure this is hard evidence, but when we saw Amber yesterday, it was pretty obvious she's had some enhancement. Seeing her jogged my memory, and I remembered this check. This points a finger at Casey—"

"I can't believe Casey would do this!" exclaimed Fred. He sputtered, "Oh, my god! This just gets worse and worse! My own brother?"

"It looks that way, but maybe there's an explanation," Jack said.

Fred's face and neck were turning crimson. "That son of a bitch! He's treated this company like his own personal play toy for years. This is just the icing on the cake! I'm going to have it out with that arrogant bastard right now!"

Fred turned on his heel and stormed out, heading for Casey's office. Casey, as was so often the case, was not in. Fred pulled out his cell phone and placed a call. "Casey! Where the hell are you?"

"I'm heading out to lunch with a potential customer. What's got you all hot under the collar?"

"We know about the checks," Fred said in a low, dangerous tone.

"Checks? What are you talking about?"

"The check made out to Plastic Surgery Associates for Amber's boob job, you son of a bitch!"

"Now hold on a minute, Fred! I can explain that."

"You've got a lot of explaining to do!" Fred said. "So it was you writing all those checks! What happened? You let yourself get into gambling debt again? You're the most irresponsible son of a bitch I know!"

"You just wait one damn minute, Fred! OK, I admit the check for the boob job was me, but that's it! I didn't write any of those other checks! You can't point the finger at me for all that other mess!"

"Casey, you must think I'm a damn fool! Where there's smoke, there's fire. You've already admitted writing one company check for personal use! Now you tell me your hands are clean on all the rest?"

"That's exactly what I'm telling you!" Casey thundered righteously. "I'm no thief! I intended to pay that $5,800 back before now. I've just been a little short lately, and I promised Amber she could get the surgery done right after Christmas."

"That's no excuse for misappropriating company funds! Get your ass down here as soon as your meeting is over—we need to talk!"

"All right, Fred. Calm down! I can try to explain things. As God is my witness, I assure you nothing like this has ever happened before or will again."

"You're damn right it won't!" said Fred as he terminated the call.

Catherine, freshly showered and dressed stylishly as usual after her house cleaning expedition, came into the office. She met her dad in the parking lot.

Casey said, "Hi, honey. I guess you've heard?"

Catherine replied, "I saw what Jack found, but I didn't want to believe my eyes! Tell me it's not true, Dad!"

"It's true. I screwed up, and I feel terrible about it. Fred and I have already had one blowup, and I think I'm heading into another one now. I didn't mean any harm. I thought...well, I thought it could be like a short-term loan."

"Dad, if you needed a short-term loan, I'm sure Uncle Fred and Aunt Velma would've been happy to help out. You didn't have to do it in a sneaky, underhanded way!"

"I know, sweetie, you're right," Casey said dejectedly. "I feel about two inches tall right now. I guess I knew I could get caught, but I really thought I'd repay the money in a few weeks and Amos could just sweep the whole thing under the rug."

"Amos was part of this?" Catherine asked.

"Yes, Amos knew. I hope I'm not getting him in trouble, too!"

"He ought to be in trouble!" Catherine said. "Amos is supposed to be a steward of the company's money; he should never get caught up in any shenanigans like this!"

"Well, I guess I screwed up there, too," Casey mumbled. "I sure have made a mess of things. I'm so sorry, sweetie." He looked down at Catherine with tears welling in his eyes. "I've made plenty of mistakes in my life, but I never wanted to do anything that made me seem small or weak in your view! Are you disgusted with me?"

"You're not exactly my knight in shining armor just now," said Catherine. "But I love you! Let's see how we can make the best of this and set things right." They walked into the building together.

Hearing Casey enter, Fred dashed down the corridor to intercept him. "Casey, in a half hour we're going to have a "come to Jesus" meeting. Be in the conference room at one thirty."

"I'll be there, Fred," Casey said dejectedly.

At the appointed time, Casey walked into the conference room. Fred, Velma, Jack, and Amos were all present. Catherine had spoken with Fred, and they both agreed it would be best for her to excuse herself from this particular meeting.

"All right, Casey," Fred led off. "You know what we're here to talk about! What the hell's going on?"

"Everyone, I feel terrible about this! I really do! I got a little behind on cash...the truth is, I had a few gambling setbacks during football season, and I promised Amber this procedure as a Christmas present. I just needed a short-term loan, and I figured the company was the best place to get it. This has never happened before in all my years, and I promise—I swear—it'll never happen again!"

"Casey, how could you?" exclaimed Velma. Jack looked stricken.

"And what's your role in this, Amos?" Fred asked icily.

"Well, I knew about it, if that's what you mean," mumbled Amos. "My job here is to do what family members tell me. I don't question a member of the Dobach family when they tell me to do something."

"Amos, your loyalty to the family is commendable, but your job is to be the guardian of our company's money, not to be a bank teller handing out money to the next guy in line," said Jack.

"I've been here almost as long as you've been alive, Jack!" said Amos pointedly. "I don't need a lecture from you on what my job is!"

"I think you do, Amos!" Velma interjected. Her eyes were red, her hair was a mess, her clothes were rumpled, and she looked like she hadn't slept in days. "You know better! You should've come to me as your supervisor and let me know what Casey was trying to do. I would've taken care of things like I always do."

"Leon Dobach told me to never question a member of the family, and I never have." Amos said righteously. "Maybe that's not part of my job description, but that's the way Leon wanted it, and that's the way I've always done it."

"We still have problems," said Fred ominously. "There is still about $60,000 in missing funds. What do you have to say about that, Casey?"

"I already told you that this was the only time I've ever stuck my hand in the till! I don't know what happened with all that other money."

"Amos, what do you have to say?"

"I can say with one hundred percent certainty that the only check I knew anything about was the one for Casey," Amos replied defensively.

"I guess you understand why it's hard for us to accept your words at face value, fellows, don't you?" asked Fred.

"You've got Mr. Ivy League MBA snooping around and trying to get to the bottom of things, right?" retorted Casey. "What have you found, Jack?"

"This is the only check I found that is directly traceable to you. The rest of the checks were made out to what look like dummy vendors and supplier companies so they could easily slip through the cracks. All the other checks were cut using automated signatures."

There was a chilly silence in the room.

Fred said, "Casey, by god, if this ever happens again, it will be the worst day you've ever lived! And, Amos, you're on a short leash as well!"

"Brother—all of you—I owe you my sincere apology. This is the worst day of my life, and I'm sorry I let you all down. I'm embarrassed and humiliated. I can tell you this has never happened before, and it will never happen again. I really regret what I did, and I'll be a changed man from now on, you'll see."

"How are you going to pay it back, Casey? And when?" Fred demanded.

"I'm OK with money right now. I'll pay it back as soon as I walk down the hall and get my checkbook," Casey replied quietly.

"Make sure you do!" Fred instructed.

Velma looked at her watch. "If we're about done here, I'd like to get back to the hospital."

"How's everything with Addie?" Fred asked.

"No real change. We're just hoping and praying she'll come around soon and she'll be all right," Velma responded in an exhausted voice.

"Aunt Velma, there's more," Jack stated quietly.

"What is it?" Velma asked. "I really need to get back to Addie."

"This concerns Addie. The checks made out to the dummy vendors…Addie approved them."

"Just what are you saying, Jack? Are you accusing Addie of something? Now? While she's unconscious in the hospital?" Velma replied shrilly.

"I'm no detective," Jack explained, "But about two and half years ago, these checks made out to dummy companies started appearing. At first, they were pretty small—only a few hundred dollars. As time passed, they got larger. Recently, there were some approaching $5,000. I've looked into our financial controls, and they're pretty weak. Addie was able to make deposits and sign checks, had access to both AR and AP, and conducted virtually all our banking transactions. And the total amount of missing money is more than we thought: it is nearly $100,000!"

"Wait a minute!" interjected Amos. "We have the same system Leon had when I got here, and it's always worked—"

"Shut your mouth, Amos!" Casey bellowed. "This is important and not a time for your whining!"

Amos's face turned red instantly.

"I'm not going to sit here and listen to this nonsense!" proclaimed Velma. "I have more important things to do than to listen to ridiculous, unfounded accusations toward a poor woman who's not even here to defend herself! I wouldn't have expected this from you, Jack!"

"I don't see how he could have done any less, Vel," Fred said softly. "We did ask him to look into this. And I checked with the bank. They're probably not supposed to tell me this, but they confided in me that Addie has one checking account with a balance of almost $50,000. I don't know how she could've saved so much money on her salary."

"You two haven't gotten to the bottom of a damn thing, if you ask me!" Velma snarled. "When Addie and I get back to work, we'll do a little forensic work of our own. We'll see who has been pocketing company money!" Velma swept out of the room in a fury.

The meeting adjourned a few minutes later. "Dad," Jack said as they walked down the hallway, "we have an 'all hands on deck' meeting with Tom Hartwell next week. Do you know what to expect?"

"Not really," replied Fred in a tired voice. "I haven't gotten an agenda yet, but he'd better impress the hell out of me, or this might be the shortest project he's ever worked on! We have too much going on right now to waste one minute of our time on some pointy headed consultant!"

"I'll be sure to tell Tom to be at his best," said Jack. "He's asked for a bunch of information about the company's finances, backlog, job cost reporting, and just about anything else you can think of. And he has talked to a bunch of us on the phone asking lots of questions, so he should be quite prepared when he gets here. I hope he can get us on a good glide path to meet the bank's deadline and help us find more margins."

"If he can do those two things, he'll have my attention, that's for sure. Otherwise, we shouldn't waste any more time or money!" Fred grumbled as he went out onto the loading dock for a smoke.

VIII
May 2014

We gathered in the conference room for our big meeting with Tom Hartwell. Velma and Addie, for obvious reasons, didn't attend, but Arthur sat in as their representative. Also present were Fred, Casey, Larry, Amos, Jack, Catherine, and Tyler. Tom called the meeting to order.

"It seems to me," Tom began, "that the first order of business is to get a forward-looking business plan submitted to and approved by the bank. What's the deadline on that?"

"They haven't given us a specific date," Jack said. "But our meeting with them was on March 10. A ninety-day deadline would mean we should have something in their hands by June 10. And that's less than six weeks away."

"That's a tight deadline, all right," Tom said dryly.

Amos spoke up. "I thought I was supposed to be in charge of this business plan, Fred! What's going on here?"

"Tell us, Amos, how is your plan coming along?" Casey inquired.

"Well, you know I've been swamped with tax preparation and all my other duties, but I've been reading up a little bit on how to do business plans, and I intended to start first thing next week."

"Amos, we don't have time for your foolishness!" Casey barked. "You've had six weeks to begin this project, but you haven't done a damn thing, and the clock has been ticking the whole time! We hired this man who has the specific expertise we need to produce a business plan without having to read a whole bunch of how-to books. We don't have time to listen to your complaining over your stupid turf! Why don't you just sit there and be quiet!"

Amos plaintively looked at Fred, who just shrugged his shoulders and spread his hands wide in a placating gesture.

Tom continued. "In order to get everything done quickly and efficiently, we're going to have to divide up responsibilities. I'll be in charge of pulling together the various components of the plan and ramrodding the first draft for presentation to the bank. Is this the group that's going to make up the Strategic Planning Project Team—which we'll abbreviate as SPPT?"

Fred said, "Yes, but Velma and Addie need to be added. Arthur is representing them today."

Arthur nodded his head toward Tom in acknowledgment.

"Great!" said Tom. "Now let's start by reviewing the company's mission statement to make sure it reflects today's thinking and realities."

Everyone referred to the Dobach Mechanical mission statement Tom projected onto the screen, and some lively conversation ensued as Tom plunged them right into the planning process.

After about thirty minutes of back and forth, Tom said, "The main thing the bank is going to want to see, in addition to up-to-date financials, is forward-looking numbers."

"Anybody can just make up a bunch of numbers and put them in a spreadsheet," Amos grumbled.

"I suppose that's true, Amos. But what we're going to do is put together realistic projections, which we'll use for future budgeting. We'll also use the *pro forma* numbers for modeling various 'what if?' scenarios. What happens if we get that next big job? What happens if we lose money on a current job? What if we buy that new machine for the sheet metal division? And so on."

"Do you have some kind of crystal ball that you can peer into and assure us these numbers are going to be right?" Amos sneered.

"Of course not! Who's ever been able to create a perfect budget where all the numbers match up for a project much less an enterprise? What an absurd thing to ask! Everyone, I'm telling you the bank wants to see *pro forma* numbers so they can be assured that we fully and complete grasp the company's finances and cash flows. Then it's up to us, the people in this room, to make the numbers work!"

He went on: "One of the reasons I collected historical income statements and balance sheets was because I wanted to be able to benchmark your financial performance against other mechanical contractors around the country. A couple of things popped up right away. Your general and administrative costs—we usually just abbreviate by saying G&A—are about twice as much as comparable mechanicals. That's an area we need to look into; there may be some real cost savings there.

"The second thing I noticed was a good bit of property on the balance sheet. It's listed at cost, of course, but even so, it looks like the company owns almost $1 million in real estate."

"That's right," Casey said. "We bought some lots a few years ago inside Dobach Mechanical because we didn't have the borrowing capacity in any of our other real estate entities. It was just too good a deal to pass up, so we did it that way."

"What's the property worth now?" asked Fred.

"Well," Casey said, "it may have appreciated a little bit, so it's probably worth about what we paid for it plus around ten percent. I was planning to hold onto it for a few more years. I know those lots are going to fetch a big price one day!"

"Is the property in a desirable location?" Tom asked. "Could it be marketed and sold fairly quickly?"

"I think so, but that doesn't mean we want to sell it," Casey remarked.

"It's an underutilized asset that, if it could be sold, might generate a huge cash windfall for the company—which is exactly what the bank is going to want to see at a time like this. If you truly want to hold on to the lots, it may be possible for you to buy the property through one of your other entities or individually. If that's not feasible, selling them could be a home run for Dobach Mechanical."

"I think everything needs to be on the table, Casey," Larry said.

Jack nodded his head in agreement.

"What about rolling stock?" Tom asked. "I noticed a crane in back of the warehouse. Equipment is often an underutilized asset that might help us generate some short-term cash."

"We almost never use that crane anymore. It's probably not worth much—maybe $10,000 or $15,000," Fred said. "Selling it won't hurt us, and it would get it out of our yard."

"Good!" said Tom. "Fred, will you look into that? And Casey, will you look into putting the lots up for sale? Can both of you let me know something about progress on those two things by the end of this week?"

Both Casey and Fred assented.

"Excellent! Now if we look at your G&A costs"—Tom passed out some spreadsheets crowded with figures—"the number-one line item by far is people and the benefits associated with them. We are probably going to need to reduce head count."

"You mean layoffs?" Fred inquired.

"That's exactly what I mean. I need to give you an assignment. You need to be in a position to tell the SPPT by the end of next week who, if you had to let someone go from the office and administrative staff, would be the most expendable. Fred, will you see to that?"

"Me?" Fred's voice rose in pitch. "I don't know how we would get by with one person less in the office. I can't see any savings there. And we're not all about the money anyway. These are people you're talking about, Tom, not numbers!"

Tom replied, "I know this is hard, Fred. No one likes the idea of having to let people go."

Jack spoke up. "I know firsthand that big companies don't think that way, Dad. And if we're gonna live to fight another day, we're going to have to make some hard, even heart-wrenching decisions. Maybe I could look at our office staff and make some recommendations to you and the SPPT. I'll start on a short process mapping assignment so we can see how AR, AP, and paper flows through the office. Once we know that, we can assess if there are inefficiencies we can eliminate. And if we reduce inefficiencies, we will know better where it is feasible to reduce head count."

"OK, just do it," Fred said glumly.

"I'm with Fred," Amos said. "With Velma and Addie out, it's putting a strain on us. In fact, I was thinking about hiring some temporary help."

"That's a nonstarter, Amos, I'm afraid," Tom said gravely. "We should put a moratorium on hiring and any large purchases of equipment or anything else not directly related to producing profits on the jobs. In addition to reducing head count, I'm also going to recommend that we cut compensation for salaried people by ten percent until we get through this crisis. We can use our *pro formas* to model and predict when we'll be able to restore everyone's foregone wages. Doing all these things will allow us to formulate a plan that's cash rich and much leaner on the expense side than that which we have right now."

Tom went on. "One large, recurring expense I noticed that also impacts both the balance sheet and income statement is the cash-value life insurance that Fred, Velma, and Casey have to fund the buy-sell agreement. When was the last time you had those insurance policies audited?"

"You mean audited like we do our annual accounting?" Amos asked.

"No, I mean audited by an insurance professional who can tell you the status of those policies and provide options for you. Do you really need to be spending $50,000 a year to support the policies, or is there sufficient cash value in them so they can be self-supporting without further outlays, even for just a few years? On the balance sheet, you have an amazing amount of cash value built up. Have you ever thought about harvesting some of that cash in the form of policy loans? We need someone to do some innovative thinking about those insurance policies—do you have a guy you can rely on? Insurance seems like a simple financial product, but when you get into the nuts and bolts of it, it is super complicated."

"Not really," responded Fred. "We've had a number of different agents over the years, each claiming to be smarter and better than the last. I'm not sure any of them have the sophistication to do the kind of analysis you're talking about."

"OK," Tom said. "If it's OK with you, I'll send the information to a person I know who is amazingly creative in situations like this. He'll probably be able to let us know something in a couple of weeks."

"You're talking lots of changes at one time!" Fred exclaimed. "We've never done anything like this on such a large scale so rapidly. Can we slow down a little bit and do things one at a time to see how they work before we move on to the next initiative?"

Amos grumbled under his breath, "You tell him, Fred!"

"Fred, I understand exactly where you're coming from," Tom said. "We just don't have the luxury of time with a six-week deadline breathing down our necks. Let's refer back to the Change Model I showed you in our previous meeting." With that, Tom projected the Change Model graphic on the conference room wall. "There were two Catalysts or foreign elements introduced to you recently. The first was the unexpected news from the bank and bonding company that they were putting you under the magnifying glass. The second was me. Having been introduced to two Catalysts, you are concerned, and rightfully so, about the upcoming period of Chaos.

"Chaos will make you feel out of balance. It's scary, unpredictable, and confusing. It's almost the polar opposite of the Status

Quo, where things are familiar and warm. You can expect the period of Chaos to be characterized by fits and starts, ups and downs, and joy and despair. You'll go through a wide range of emotions ranging from optimism to intense negativity—sometimes on the same day. Our goal, of course, is to move beyond Chaos as quickly as possible by introducing a Transforming Idea or two, then Integrating the ideas, and then Practicing them and getting you to a New Status Quo. The whole point is to make you and Dobach Mechanical better than you were before by introducing new ways of looking at yourselves and your business. This project will be a lot of fun, but it also will be emotionally exhausting."

"Tom, all that emotional turmoil is the last thing this family needs with Addie's situation!" said Fred.

"Fred, he is on the right path," Larry asserted. "We've been successful for a long time, and even the recession didn't change too much around here. We're probably ready for a little bit of reinvention and improvement. Maybe this bank thing will turn out to have been good for us in the long run."

"I just know I have a huge amount of work on my desk, and I don't have time for a lot of meetings," said Tyler.

"Good observation, Tyler," Tom said. "Everybody's going to need to buckle down. Your normal workload isn't going to go down one bit, and this project will, in all likelihood, add to it. It's of vital importance, and the very survival of your company could hinge on it. It's going to require a dedicated, concerted effort from everyone here."

"I'm not too overloaded, Tom," Jack said. "I can help out quite a bit."

"Me too!" said Catherine.

"Great! We're going to need everyone's help," Tom continued. "My recommendations are: first, reduce head count in the office with the least possible disruption; second, cut G&A salaries ten percent across the board; third, move with all deliberate speed to sell those undeveloped lots and the crane; and fourth, have my insurance guy make recommendations to save some money. Does everyone understand their assignments?"

Everyone said they did.

Arthur spoke up for the first time. "I didn't really know what to expect when Velma asked me to attend in her place. I have to admit that I was a little skeptical. But I think you've come up with some excellent, actionable ideas for how to get this company back in the pink of health, Tom. If we all buckle down together as a team and take his advice, we'll come out of this thing stronger than ever!"

"That's the goal, Arthur!" Tom said. "Are there any other comments or takeaways? All right then, everyone has their assignments! Let's get to work!"

Just then, Arthur's cell phone rang. It was Velma. "Honey, get down here right away! Addie's awake!"

"I'm on my way," Arthur said as he raced for the door.

IX

May 2014

Our second business planning meeting was coming up, and all were cautiously optimistic. The agenda for today had us doing something called a SWOT analysis (strengths, weaknesses, opportunities, and threats), plus a review of our primary competition. The business planning process was beginning to flow, and we thought we just might be getting the hang of it.

Fred and Jack were having breakfast at a local greasy spoon prior to starting the workday.

"I'm glad Addie's awake and alert," said Jack. "That's got to be a relief for Velma and Arthur."

"It sure is," said Fred. "We don't exactly know what her condition is yet, but at least she's conscious and interacting with the doctors and nurses."

"What happens next?" asked Jack.

"I don't know," Fred replied. "I expect they'll move her out of intensive care. We'll have to wait for word from Velma."

"What happens next at work?"

"That's kind of a problem, too. All things seem to point to Addie, and the CPAs agree with your assessment, Jack. But Velma didn't take the news very well. And I guess there's still a sliver of doubt in my mind, too. Could it have been someone else? Could it have been Amos?"

"Amos hasn't got the courage to do something so brazen. And I think he would have been a little cleverer about hiding his tracks. Dad, it's almost like Addie wanted to get caught. What Catherine said about the condition of her house and then this; I don't think anyone really understood Addie's state of mind."

"You can say that again," said Fred. "We should have been more alert and sensitive, I suppose. You going to eat that biscuit?"

"No, you can have it. I don't think my stomach can take any more of this. So do you have any idea what we're going to do about Addie and Velma? I know you're not going to get the authorities involved in this, but at the same time we can't just have Addie waltz right back into her old job and put ourselves in a vulnerable position again."

"Son, I don't know what to do. We've never had to deal with anything like this before. Maybe Tom Hartwell has some ideas. We should probably head on back so we're there in time for the meeting."

"Separate checks?" the waitress asked.

"I've got it," said Fred.

In the family's second formal, "all hands on deck" meeting with Tom, the group again met in the conference room. Fred, Velma—looking much more herself—Casey, Jack, Tyler, Catherine, Heath, Amos, and Larry were present. Tom had spent a few minutes privately before the meeting with Velma, and they were the last to file in.

"OK, let's get status reports from everybody, starting with Casey and the commercial property," Tom said, kicking off the proceedings.

"I got the lots listed with our brokerage guy, and he's pretty optimistic that he can get these things moved within the next sixty to ninety days. We've listed them for right at $1 million, and he thinks that's a pretty fair figure."

"That's great news! Well done, Casey!" said Tom. Casey bowed his head slightly at Tom in recognition of the pat on the back. "This will make a big difference in our *pro forma* balance sheet!"

"I still think that property is going to be a home run for somebody," Casey groaned.

"Maybe so, Casey," interjected Fred. "But it's not going to be us! We've got bigger fish to fry right now."

"What about the crane, Fred?" asked Tom.

"I sold it to a buddy in South Carolina," Fred reported proudly. "I got $17,000 for it, too! He's already taken possession. You didn't see it cluttering up our yard this morning, did you?"

"Good work, Fred! That's the kind of thinking and action we need. Jack, what have you developed about potentially reducing office head count?"

Jack passed out some spreadsheets and something that looked like a complicated flow chart. "I've spent time doing process mapping on the typical office functions: invoice processing and approval, submittals, check writing, and even things like balancing bank accounts. I believe we have some inefficiencies and redundancies that could be eliminated. For example, look at page two—"

Jack detailed his proposed changes for about fifteen minutes. "The bottom line is, I think we can eliminate two full-time positions and make another part-time. The savings should be over $120,000 per year when factoring benefits into the equation."

"Great work Jack!" Tom exclaimed. Others in the room, also impressed with Jack's analysis, smiled and nodded their encouragement.

"I think we need to be careful about this issue of letting people go," said Fred sternly. "How do you propose we do this without destroying morale and inducing a fear that the ship is sinking and we're all panicking?"

"Great question, Fred," Tom replied, "We have to expect some pushback whenever there's a reduction in force. Furthermore, we need to have a plan for how we're going to 'sell' this"—Tom made an air quotes gesture—"to the rest of the employees. We don't want the reduction in head count to be a horrible morale buster, so it must be presented in the best light possible."

Catherine spoke up. "I was concerned about that, too. I'm glad to hear we're going to develop a plan for finding the positive side of this. I'd like to help with that aspect."

"Excellent, Catherine. Thank you," said Tom. "Larry, if we can generate this kind of savings in the office, what about in the field?"

"To tell the truth, Tom, I've been thinking about that. I think there is a little room for right-sizing our field crews and mechanics."

"Barney Smith from First National called me yesterday," Fred interrupted. "He wanted to know how we were coming along in light of our deadline next month."

"What did you tell him?" Velma asked.

"I told him that we'd hired Tom Hartwell here and that we're taking aggressive steps to meet their deadline. He seemed pleased. He knew of Tom through his work at Allen's company as well as by reputation from some other assignments. Tom, you must be kind of a big deal!" Fred said with a hint of sarcasm.

"I don't know about that," Tom replied. "I'm glad Barney and First National have a good opinion of me! That can't hurt us."

"Tom, it seems like things are moving pretty quickly, and we're making progress on a number of fronts, but there's an issue I'd like to raise," said Velma sternly.

"Of course, go right ahead."

"There've been some allegations about Addie being responsible for those missing funds, and it came from Fred and Jack. I think we need to address this. I don't think it's fair at all for them to gang up and point the finger at Addie! We know for a fact that Casey has been doing the very thing Addie is accused of!"

Casey, Catherine, and Amos shifted in their chairs uncomfortably.

"Thanks for bringing that up, Velma," said Tom. "I'm not sure we're in a position to know exactly what happened and who is responsible. However, Velma and everyone else, you have to keep your minds open and be realistic. Addie may very well have had something to do with this. On the other hand, maybe she didn't. What I propose to do, if it's all right with everyone, is to look at the material Jack has assembled and meet with your CPA and banker for just a few hours. I don't want to run up any unnecessary professional fees, but they'll help with objectivity and experience. Together we will determine a crystal-clear picture of what happened. Until then, I suggest we don't make any other accusations against family members or anyone else. And I'd like for you, Fred, Jack, and Casey to call a truce among yourselves. We've got two health improvement projects going on here: one is the Dobach family, and the other is Dobach Mechanical. How's that sound?"

"It sounds perfectly rational to me," said Velma. "Maybe we should have been more deliberate the first time before we started throwing accusations about!"

"I hope what I found is incorrect, Velma," said Jack. "Maybe Tom and the others will find some new information and we can clear everybody."

"I'm sure that'll be the case!" Velma sniffed.

The group then began to focus on Tom as he stuck five large sheets of paper to the conference room wall and labeled them: Strengths, Weaknesses, Opportunities, Threats, and Barriers. "We call this a SWOT-B exercise," Tom explained. "We'll analyze each and brainstorm for about fifteen minutes for each item. This will give us the raw material we need to begin to develop priorities for action, our big-picture goals for the next thirty-six months, and our shorter-term goals. Let's dig in."

The group got to work energetically.

"All right, excellent!" Tom said after a couple of hours of work. "We're about wrapped up here for the morning. I'm going to meet with Jack, Larry, Casey, and Catherine so we can look at the current backlog and put together our revenue projections for the rest of this year and then 2015 through 2017."

"I've got some good news there!" Casey said excitedly. "You all know I've been wining and dining the developer behind that big mall project. The mechanical package for the mall and outparcels is about $17 million, and it looks like we've got it!"

"That's great news, Casey!" exclaimed Tom. "That's a very positive development!"

"When would you expect to go to contract?" asked Fred.

"That might still be a few weeks off, but I'd say it's about ninety-eight percent in the bag," Casey replied. "We also know who's going to be the architect and general contractor; we've partnered with both of them a bunch of times. Looks like it'll be a really nice six-month project."

"Terrific, Casey!" Larry said happily. "Nice work!"

Casey beamed. Catherine reached over discreetly and patted her dad's hand with a lovely smile of encouragement.

Tyler piped up: "I have something to say, Tom, before you steal Larry away for your meeting. I need to meet with him and Fred to go over one of my projects. It's getting a little sideways, and I think we need to dig in and take a look at it."

"Tyler, thanks for bringing that up," encouraged Tom. "I think we're wrapped up here. Fred and Larry, why don't we meet with Tyler right now?"

Most of the group left the room, leaving just Fred, Larry, Tyler, and Tom. Tyler pulled out a stack of job cost reports and plans, and shared them. Larry adjusted his reading glasses and began to go over the numbers.

"This is getting a little dicey," Larry said. "And these are the March month-end numbers. Haven't you got April yet? Crap, it's almost the end of May!"

"Amos hasn't gotten me the April report yet, but I can tell you it's not going to look good."

"Jesus Christ, son!" Fred shouted. "Why did you wait until now to bring this to Larry and me? We could lose hundreds of thousands of dollars on this job if we can't get it turned around!"

"I know, Dad," Tyler said steadily. "That's why we're talking."

"I just don't understand you," Fred exclaimed. "Some of your jobs are home runs and others are absolute dogs. There's no middle ground with you. Can't you just hit singles and doubles sometimes? Has it always got to be feast or famine?"

Tyler reddened. "By god, I am sick and tired of all the damn criticism around here! There's never an 'attaboy' or 'job well done'. It's always 'you screwed up' or 'what have you done for me lately'! This is bullshit! I try and get help to put this job back on an even keel, and all you want to do is criticize! I bet a lot of companies would like to have a project manager with my track record! I bet I could make more money working somewhere else, too!"

"Tyler," Tom interjected, "emotions are running a little high here, and I'd hate to hear either one of you say anything you'll regret later. Why don't each of you take a five-minute time-out, get a cup of coffee, cool down, and come on back so we can break this project down and figure out how to put it back together again?"

Tyler angrily looked at his father. "I'll take a five-minute break all right! I'll see you guys tomorrow—maybe!" Tyler stalked out and slammed the door behind him.

"Larry, can you roll up your sleeves and get a handle on this thing?" Fred asked, shaking his head sadly.

"Let me take a closer look at it. I'll pull in—quietly—another PM and superintendent to help me. I'll be able to let you know something tomorrow."

"That's great," said Fred. Tom nodded his head. "And, Tom, what advice have you got for me about Tyler? What should I do?"

"I'll call him later this afternoon once he's had a chance to cool down. Maybe a little third-party counseling will go a long way."

"I sure hope so!" Fred said. "He's always either hot or cold; there is no in between. And I suppose you know about his past history of alcohol and drug use. Do you think that might be an issue again?"

"I'm no expert on that subject," Tom said. "What's your company's drug-testing policy?"

Fred and Larry proceeded to give Tom a rundown, and the three developed a plan for assessing Tyler and getting him back into the fold. Tom and Larry then began to prepare for their next session.

At the end of the day, Fred left the office and arrived at his comfortable, well-appointed home. He parked his car, closed the garage door, and walked into the kitchen, where he prepared himself a drink. Daphne walked in.

"I want you to tell me what the hell happened today!" she demanded.

"What? What are we talking about?"

"What happened between you and Tyler? He said you treated him like a dog and threatened to fire him!" Tears began to roll down Daphne's cheeks. "Tyler needs this job, Fred! He might not be able to work anywhere else! You can't abuse him like this; I won't have it! If you let him go, I don't...I don't...I don't know what I'll do!"

"Hold on a minute, honey!" said Fred. "That's not exactly the way it happened. You got one side of the story; let me tell you mine." Fred, in a calm and measured voice, gave his less melodramatic version of the events of the day. "The bottom line is, one of Tyler's projects might cost the company a million dollars—and this isn't the first time. Tyler does a great job on some projects and absolutely screws the pooch on others. We can't just ignore the fact that his performance is inconsistent. I wonder if he might have slipped back into his old habits."

"Why do you even say that, Fred? He's been clean for years now, and you know that!"

"Daphne, honey, we don't know anything. We've always exempted family members from company drug testing, but I'm not sure that's a wise move anymore."

"I will not have my son drug tested like a common criminal!" Daphne shouted. "What kind of message does that send to your own son?"

"First of all, we don't know exactly what we're going to do yet. Second, I hope it would send a message that we're beginning to hold family members—me included—more accountable for their performance at Dobach Mechanical."

"Well, I don't care what you do as long as Tyler has a good job and can make a good living! You've got a grandson to think about, too—don't forget that!"

"I haven't forgotten, sweetie. I'm sorry to have you in the middle of all this. We'll get it worked out."

"I certainly hope so! I guess you can pull together your own dinner tonight can't you?" Daphne asked as she slammed the door behind her.

"I guess so," Fred said wearily as he searched his pockets for a cigarette.

X

May 2014

We were making progress on our business plan, but we only had a month before we needed to meet with the bank. Time was not our ally, and in terms of the Change Model Tom had introduced, it seemed like we would never move beyond Chaos.

"Thanks for meeting with me, Tyler. I appreciate that you consented, me being fairly new to you all, to talking about your future."

"You're welcome, Tom. I don't know who to talk to! Inside my own family I don't feel like I'm ever heard."

"Tell me more, Tyler."

"Well, Jack's the golden boy. He was always the perfect son. Now he's the perfect dad and husband. He and Angie are both high achievers and go-getters. I've never compared well with my brother; Dad in particular always identified more with Jack than me. Throw in my failure to finish college, drug and alcohol problems, divorce, and the occasional money-losing project at work, and I'm just a black sheep. It ain't a pretty comparison when you look at the two of us."

"I don't know about that. I've heard some pretty nice things. Some of your projects have made big money for the company. Your creativity and talent are also things I've heard about. Sure, you've had challenges in the past, but I think you might be selling yourself short."

"Maybe," Tyler said wearily. "All I know is that I don't hear a damn thing when I do a good job. It's always, 'What have you done for me lately?' And when I have a little problem, it's like the world is coming to an end. And I think I get paid the least among all the PMs on my team. I don't know why I stay. I feel miserable most of the time. Working in Granddad's and Dad's shadows—and now Jack's—might be more than I want to put up with."

"If it's not too forward, Tyler, let me suggest an idea. First, I am not, repeat *not*, advising you to leave the family business. I can't emphasize that enough. However, think about this. What harm would there be in putting your résumé out there? Lots of contractors are looking for experienced project managers as the economy recovers; it can't hurt to see what's available in the job market. That way, you'll have choices. If it looks like you have more opportunity for happiness with another company, you'd have the option to pursue that. On the other hand, you might consider your alternatives and determine that staying with the family business isn't as bad as you thought. You'd have choices and good information on which to evaluate alternatives, and that's almost always a good thing. You've never worked anywhere else, have you?"

"No, I haven't. I've always wondered if I would do better at a place where I'd be judged solely as an employee and not as the son of the boss or a member of the family that controls the company. A thought just occurred to me: if I did leave Dobach Mechanical, would I have to sell my stock back?"

"No. Your buy-sell agreement is silent on that subject. I don't necessarily think that would be an issue. But let's not put the cart before the horse. I'm not suggesting you should work elsewhere. I'm just saying you need know what the marketplace for PMs is like. You might find you don't have it so bad here in the family business once you shop around."

"Tom, you might be on to something. I'm sick and tired of being the black sheep and having Dad come down like a ton of bricks when the least little thing happens. I'm going to try and put a résumé together and look online to see what jobs might be out there. Maybe if I got a fresh start at another company, things would be different for me."

"That's a possibility. But I want to emphasize again I am *not* counseling you to jump ship. Please keep me posted."

"I will, Tom. Thanks for spending a little time with me."

Velma was helping Addie pack up her things at the hospital in preparation for her discharge; Arthur was coming to pick them up in a few minutes. "Libbie, Lisa, and Catherine did a great job cleaning up your house, Addie. You'll be returning to a much different place."

"I guess I had let it get pretty run down. I just never had any energy for housework or yard work when I came home from the office. And Stephen was always the clean freak between us."

"That's OK, Addie. You can always count on your father and me to help whenever you need us. You know we love you, don't you?"

Tears began to course down Addie's cheeks. "Mom, maybe this is a bad time...there will probably never be a good time...I don't know how to say this." Her shoulders began to shake as she sobbed.

"Honey! What is it? You can tell me! Nothing can be that bad!"

"I did it, Mom. The money. I was the one."

Addie couldn't go on; her confession left her overcome with remorse and shame.

"What are you saying, baby? Are you talking about the money at work? We're going to solve that mystery as soon as you're ready to come back. Jack and the others have another thing coming if they think they can make baseless charges against you and get away with it. I bet Amos and—"

"Mom, you're not listening! I've talked to Dr. Michaels about this, and I have to confess. I took the money. It was me and no one else."

"Addie, no!"

Velma, too, began crying. They embraced wordlessly. The nurse came in with Addie's discharge paperwork, saw the delicate situation, and respectfully withdrew. After a few minutes, Addie and her mom were again able to talk.

"Addie! This can't be true!"

"It is, Mom. I can't deny it, and I can't live with it anymore. Dr. Michaels was right. I have to confess, pay the money back, and start over with my life."

"Is that why you—"

"Yes. I felt so guilty. I've worked in the family business longer than anyone else in my generation, and then when Jack came back making almost triple what I do…well, that was too much."

"But he made so much on Wall Street!"

"Please, Mom, just listen! That's not all. Don't you think I can see what condition I let myself and my home get into? I see what a mess I made of my marriage, my relationship with my kids, and my job. I have no friends, I don't know my neighbors, and I have no hobbies. I need to reassess and start over. This is no way to live!"

"No, honey, you have lots of friends. And your father and I will stand by you every step of the way. Please come back to work!"

"Mom, you're not listening again. I need to do something on my own. You and Dad have always sheltered me, bought me things, and protected me at work, even when I was doing a crappy job. I need to find something I can feel passionate about doing and make my own way. It would be best for me to leave the family business, sell my house, pay back the money I took, and start over. Dr. Michaels has helped me see more clearly; this is something I just have to do!"

"Don't make any rash decisions, Addie. Maybe you should give yourself a few months—"

"No!" Addie exclaimed with a resolve Velma had rarely, if ever, heard from her. "I'm determined it's going to be different this time. It's past time for me to make some changes."

Catherine and Jack were working on a marketing assignment from Tom and the SPPT. She had her usual stack of books nearby; she had done an amazing amount of reading and turned herself into a business-to-business marketing expert in only a few weeks.

"These are brilliant ideas, Catherine! I think the group is going to love them. And I think, if we execute even half of the marketing plan you've laid out, we'll increase our volume by a bunch in 2015!"

"Thanks! I'm excited about it, too. But construction is still a man's world; I'm a little worried how all this will be received."

"The whole Dobach Mechanical team will be there to support you; I can guarantee that. And the plan calls for Casey and Larry to be the faces of the marketing campaign—at least for a while. That will help sell it, too. I think you're going to do great, and I think the plan is going to be great!"

"I hope so. While we're cutting the budget in so many areas, the idea of spending more money on business development is going to rub some people the wrong way. I worry they'll see it as money wasted on fluff and pointless promotion. I hope they'll understand the wisdom and necessity of changing how we have traditionally done business development and gotten work."

"Everyone's going to have to revise their opinions of how we do things. It's a new reality today. You'll do great, Catherine. You'll have them eating out of your hand," said Jack.

XI

June 2014

We were nervous about the bank meeting. Tom was going to lead the presentation; Fred, Velma, and Casey were going to support him and add context in their areas. And once the bank meeting was over, we still had to pass muster with the bonding company. Addie was home from the hospital, but we didn't know exactly what to expect or how to behave around her. We didn't want our awkwardness to push her away. One thing was for sure: the summer was off to an eventful start!

"Tom, where would you locate us on the Change Model now?" asked Catherine.

"Great question. Let's take a look." Tom projected the Change Model on the wall. "Where do you all think you are?"

"I have no idea," muttered Amos woodenly. "We've got so many balls in the air right now, I don't see how anyone can keep up with them all."

"OK, for Amos it appears he's still in Chaos. What about the rest of you?"

Jack said, "Chaos could certainly rear its head again any time, but I would say from a business point of view that we're well into the Transforming Idea stage. We are in the process of reducing head count in both the office and the field, cutting salaries and overhead, selling underutilized assets, using locked up money from those old whole life insurance policies, doing intense strategic

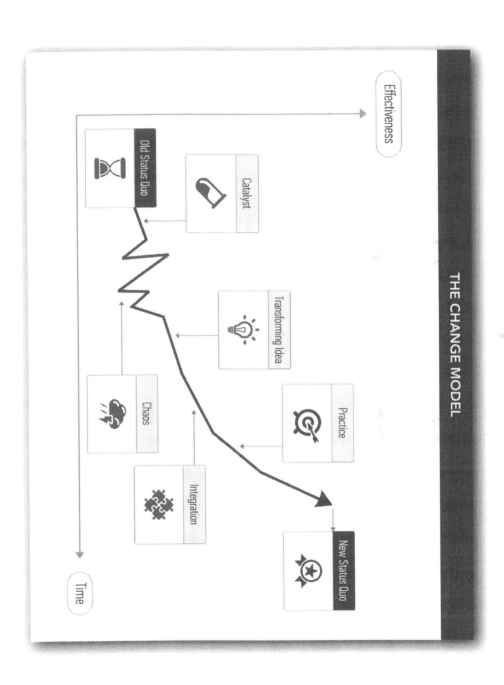

THE CHANGE MODEL

Effectiveness

Old Status Quo

Catalyst

Transforming Idea

Chaos

Practice

Integration

New Status Quo

Time

business planning, reconfiguring benefits plans, introducing our first coordinated and planned business development program, and doing forward-looking budgeting and cash flow forecasts. We've come a long way in only three months!"

"I agree," said Larry. "I can't believe how much the SPPT has been able to accomplish in such a short time. I have to confess that, before all this started, I was getting a little bored and found myself contemplating retirement at times. Now I'm as excited about our prospects at Dobach Mechanical as I was twenty-five years ago!"

"That's good to hear!" Fred exclaimed. "I get the willies every time I hear you mention retirement. I was probably the most skeptical of anyone—except maybe for Amos—when we asked Tom to help out. I don't know what First National is going to say, but, as for me, I'm really proud of all of you and the work we've done. I'm like Larry: I'm pretty charged up about where we're going!"

"Excellent feedback, everyone. Thank you," said Tom. "We've talked about the Change Model quite a bit; now it's time to shift our thinking a little bit toward change management. The conventional wisdom is that seventy percent of change initiatives in business fail, and I don't want you all to fall into that trap. You'll feel, as Leon did when he tried strategic planning, that your time and money were wasted."

Amos rolled his eyes and nodded, making it clear how little he was enjoying the process.

Tom continued. "Leon was famous for his jokes about death and taxes, but I think he left out a very important component: *change.* And I propose we add that variable to our thinking here and now. Nothing we do as a planning team is going to stick and produce long-term improvements if we don't recognize and combat the powerful urge to return to the Status Quo."

"How do we do that, Tom?" asked Catherine.

"Great question! First of all, this group"—Tom looked intently at the people around the table—"is going to have to model the changes we seek. You're going to be the change champions. You're going to be one hundred percent enthusiastic and supportive of the changes—doing more with less, the rationale for pay cuts, the need to reduce head count, etc. You can show absolutely zero chinks in the armor. You're going to walk the talk!"

Larry and Jack nodded enthusiastically. Fred seemed a little queasy. He said, "Hold on a minute, Tom! What if we have genuine questions or concerns? You don't want us to, in essence, lie to people, do you? That isn't who we are."

"No, I would never advise you to lie. I would, however, caution you about expressing your reservations around the office or anywhere that might get back to an employee or his family." Tom looked intently at Fred and Amos in turn. "Maybe we should go back to the old saying: 'If you don't have something nice to say, don't say anything at all!' Those of us engineering these changes and managing the process of adapting to the 'new normal' economic realities have to model and demonstrate that the changes are positive and that we're in charge of our own destinies."

Fred gave a brief nod.

"Through your words and actions, you're going to teach the other Dobach Mechanical employees to embrace and even like the changes we're planning. Beyond that, you're going to rally the 'early adopters,' those who see the necessity of change and embrace it first, to go out and spread the gospel of change just as you do."

Amos was squirming in his seat.

"Finally, those who absolutely cannot get up to speed with the new change and learning culture, the ones who grumble and even sabotage our efforts, will need to find another place to hang their hats."

"Come on, Tom!" Fred exclaimed. "You can't say we're going to just fire people! I'm pretty uncomfortable with some of this myself; you gonna fire me, too?"

Amos smiled for the first time since the meeting began.

Jack and Catherine spoke at almost the same time. "You go ahead, Catherine," Jack said.

"Thanks. I don't think that's exactly what he means." She looked at Tom for confirmation. Tom inclined his head toward Catherine as encouragement to continue. "This change management process is just that—a lengthy process. It wouldn't be fair to introduce a change on Monday and then on Tuesday search out anyone who is uncomfortable and cut them loose. We have to educate ourselves and, in turn, our people on the Change Model and then give them the right incentives and encouragement to adapt their work behaviors toward continuous improvement. We're adapting—very suddenly—to changes thrust upon us by the bank and bonding companies. They are the catalysts, and we have no choice but to make the changes necessary; our survival as a family business depends on it. But this could be an opportunity for us to see that, instead of something to be feared and dreaded, change is an understandable, predictable process. That being the case, we can use the model and the change management skills I'm sure Tom is dying to teach us"—Tom smiled in acknowledgement—"to identify and implement new ideas and tools long after the bank crisis is behind us. But all that depends on us walking the walk and teaching other team members to do the same. Ultimately, those who don't get it or can't go along with our new, improved learning culture would be happier and better off working elsewhere. And we'll be happier and better off if we can identify and hire people who are eager to embrace our new culture."

"Good, Catherine! You said what I was trying to say much more clearly," Tom stated. "Thanks for making me look good!" She smiled sheepishly.

"There's more, Tom." He gestured for her to continue. "Since you introduced the Change Model to us, I've been doing a little independent study." Catherine selected a book from her stack and held up *Switch: How to Change Things When Change is Hard* by Chip and Dan Heath. "This is a fascinating read, and it corroborates what you and Jack are saying. They make the point that we generalize the change process as *analyze-think-change*, but the reality is that successful change initiatives go more like *see-feel-change*. To make everything we're doing materialize, we should develop a separate implementation strategy so we can encourage all our people to emotionally embrace what we're doing. They will need to see how they fit into our changes and what's in it for them. Once they *feel* the value of the changes, once we can appeal to them on both the thinking and emotional levels, then we'll have full buy-in and the changes will become easier and easier."

"Outstanding, Catherine!" Tom said enthusiastically. "I'm really impressed!"

Casey beamed at his daughter. "That is really some good work, sweetie!" Catherine blushed at both the compliment and her father's term of affection.

Tom asked, "Can we assume then, Catherine, that you will be one of the point people on developing our communication strategy? It won't do for the employees to see all these meetings with a strange consultant taking place and not know what we're doing. If we don't provide the correct information and present it in the right way, the rumors will begin to circulate, and we'll have a hard time getting ahead of the curve."

"Sure," said Catherine. "And will Jack lend a hand—maybe Heath and Larry, too? All the employees respect you, Larry. I envision that your support will really make a difference."

"Why, I'd be delighted—as long as you do most of the heavy lifting, Catherine!" joked Larry.

Catherine nodded. It was easy to see how excited she was by the intellectual and practical challenges the communications strategy would present.

"Back to more pressing matters: the bank meeting is at the end of this week, so let's get focused on our financial projections and narrative, shall we?" Tom began to project components of the business plan onto the screen for discussion and deliberation.

It was a beautiful June morning in Virginia. The sun was shining, there were only scattered clouds, and the usual oppressive southern heat and humidity were nowhere to be found. Fred, Velma, Casey, and Tom pulled in at First National headquarters for their presentation. They were greeted in the conference room by Barney Smith.

"I'm not sure you've met my two colleagues," he said, and he introduced his boss, the head of the bank's credit department, and the president. There were greetings and handshakes all around. "I think we have the audio/visual equipment set up as requested. Why don't you fire up your laptop, and we'll get started?"

"Ladies and gentlemen," Fred began, rising to his feet, "we were pretty shaken when we first met with Barney in March, and we reacted, as you would've expected: defensively and apprehensively."

Velma and Casey nodded in agreement.

"However, since that time, we've taken a look at every single aspect of Dobach Mechanical and our other related businesses, and we have instituted many changes. What you're about to see represents a new direction—a renewed focus—and it has us as excited about our business as we've been in decades. In a way, we have First National to thank for it. Tom, why don't you take it from here?"

"Thanks, Fred. As you know, the Dobach family asked me for a small assist on this business plan project. Let me first direct your attention to—" Tom was off and running with the presentation. Two hours later, the conference room doors opened, everyone shook hands, and the meeting was done.

The presenters arrived back at Dobach Mechanical just before noon. Seeing them in the parking lot, Jack, Catherine, Larry, and Heath met them at the door with wide eyes. "How did it go?" Catherine and Jack blurted at almost the same time.

Fred answered, "Well, that remains to be seen. They'll need some time to review the plan thoroughly and examine the numbers. But judging from their reactions and what the president of the bank said to us as we were leaving, I think the presentation couldn't have gone much better. He told me that it was the most thorough, well-thought-out, and impressive business plan he'd seen in thirty years." Fred looked relieved as he fished in his pocket for a cigarette.

"Way to soft-sell it, Fred!" Casey chortled. "We blew their asses away. Tom knocked their butts in the dirt. He had their questions answered before they even thought them up. Those guys went from threatening to jerk our line of credit to practically slobbering all over us. I'm surprised they didn't offer us their firstborn children before we made it out the door."

"It went well, very well. Casey, as always"—Velma gave him a sideways glance—"is overstating things some. But it really did feel like we gave them everything they wanted and more. I don't think they're ready to take us off their watch list yet, but the pressure is definitely on the way down. I'm so relieved!"

"Wow! That's great!" exclaimed Jack. "What happens next?"

"Next week we do it all over again for the damn bonding company," chuckled Casey.

"Let's go make ourselves more comfortable in the conference room and talk this out a little," suggested Velma.

The group had an excited, energetic fifteen-minute conversation. Jack, Catherine, Larry, and Heath wanted to hear every detail about the comments the bankers had made.

"Changing the subject a bit, I have some news," Velma related. "Addie, Arthur, and I have been meeting with Dr. Michaels since she left the hospital. We have been thinking about a lot of things, and we've come to some important decisions." Everyone leaned toward Velma in rapt attention. Her voice quavered a bit as she continued. "It was Addie who took the missing money after all. I still can't believe it, but it's true." There were a few murmurs; Velma held up her hand for silence. "Addie is selling her house. She's going to repay every dime she took."

"Velma, I don't know—"

"Forget it, Fred. This is what Addie wants, and it's the right thing to do. If she were here, she would extend her deepest apologies and beg you all for forgiveness. I too ask for your forgiveness; I should've known. I should have been able to see her state of mind and head this off. My own daughter!" Velma's eyes filled with tears, and she looked down at the floor.

"Come on, Vel," Casey said softly. "No one knew. Who would've thought any of us—" Casey, suddenly aware of his own recent fiasco with the company checkbook, lapsed into an embarrassed silence.

"Addie won't be coming back to her old job. And as soon as we find a replacement for me, I'm retiring, too."

"Wait a minute! This is all so sudden!" said Fred. "Are you sure? Addie might do well in an old, comfortable environment. And we wouldn't want to lose you, too!"

"This is how it's going to be, Fred. Tom, you can add back Addie's former salary, modest as it was, to your financial projections. And my replacement won't likely cost the company as much as me, so that will be another financial windfall."

"The numbers will take care of themselves, Velma," said Tom. "I just want you to be sure you have given this adequate consideration— Addie, too—and that you won't regret anything you've decided."

"We won't. Assuming the meeting with the bonding company goes as well next week as this one today, we should start looking for my replacement right away. Arthur is cutting back, too; we'll be spending a lot more time at the beach. As long as we're changing things around here, we might as well get rid of some old blood and bring in some new."

Jack and Catherine gave their aunt hugs as the meeting broke up. For the moment, it appeared that the potential working capital crisis had been averted, and while there were plenty of changes to assimilate, Dobach Mechanical had a sound, inspiring plan for the next three years.

That evening, Fred was home a little after four o'clock, a cigarette and drink in hand as usual. He walked into the den as happy as he'd been in a long time. He was really pleased with how the family management team had rallied to meet this crisis situation and overcome it so handily. He pulled up short, a little startled. Daphne was sitting quietly in the den and staring at him stonily. She looked as if she'd been crying.

"I guess you heard?"

"Heard what?" Fred asked.

"Tyler has taken a job in Georgia! He's leaving home! And it's that damn consultant's fault!"

XII
July 2014

With the bank crisis averted, at least for now, we thought we could breathe a sigh of relief and go back to business as usual. That wasn't to be the case. Just as one period of Chaos drew to a close, another one took its place.

The bank had asked for submission of quarterly cash flow projections, and Jack and Tom were attempting to get Amos to understand not only how to produce them but why the report had value beyond mere compliance.

"We've never had to do these before; I don't see why we need to start now," groaned Amos.

"Think of it this way, Amos. Now instead of financials that tell us how we did last month or last year, we have a tool that will help us look ahead and plan for the future! You won't be just a historian anymore; you'll be a forecaster!" explained Tom.

"That's right, Amos," Jack added. "If we can predict what future cash flows will be, we'll be able to schedule with more precision our debt repayment, capital expenditures, bonuses, and everything else. You've said yourself that the first quarter of every year is scary because we have tax distributions, employee bonuses, retirement plan contributions, and property taxes all due during our slowest revenue quarter of the year. Using this tool, we will be able to get ahead of that cash drain, and things will be less tight and stressful."

"As I said before; anyone can plug numbers into a spreadsheet and say they're right! This doesn't prove anything," retorted Amos.

"Ahhhh, but where will our numbers come from?" asked Tom. "We have our job budgets, right? And we know our historical G&A costs, right? And we now have enterprise-wide budgets based on those historical trends, right? These aren't made up numbers. They're approximations based on historical numbers, plus job budgets, plus reasonable forward-looking assumptions. As time goes by and we practice this process and learn more, we will get better and better at getting the numbers right. We'll have this down to a science in no time."

"I already have a ton of work to do. This is just one more thing I don't have time to get to," sniffed Amos.

"Amos, this is nonnegotiable," said Tom with a stern look. "We have to do this as a condition to maintain our credit facility. While we're at it, we might as well utilize it as a business management tool and get some value out of it."

"I'm just not comfortable doing this! I don't believe in it, and I'm worried that I might somehow be guilty of bank fraud if I send them numbers that are made up and that I don't support one hundred percent!"

Jack, exasperated, said, "OK, I've heard enough! Tom, let's talk to Dad and Uncle Casey. I have an idea on how we can get this done without Amos."

Amos stammered, "Hold on a minute! I think I see your point—"

But the two had already left his office. Amos, his stomach churning, reached for the desk drawer where he kept a bottle of antacid tablets and wondered if he'd crossed the line.

Angie and Lisa, covered in sweat, were walking out of the gym having completed another grueling early-morning workout. Lisa, toweling her short hair, said, "I hear things are really changing down at the company."

"Sounds like it to me," Angie replied. "Addie has quit—thank god she has resolved to make some changes. She sounds so determined to make a new start; I'm proud of her! Velma is resigning as soon as they find a replacement. They made some big expense cuts, reduced salaries, and landed a big new job, and they have forward-looking budgets and projected cash flows for the first time ever. Jack is pumped! He says they're now starting to run the business in a professional way, and I agree. I know a family business will never be run solely by the numbers like a public company, but I've always thought there were ways to take some of the better big-company ideas and install them into Dobach Mechanical."

"Wow! It sounds like you're more excited than Jack!"

"Maybe I am," Angie laughed. "For the first time since he started five years ago, he feels engaged and like the company is making use of his talents."

As they neared their cars, Lisa paused. "There's another change coming, I hear. Tyler told Heath, who told Libbie, who told me he was leaving, too!"

"Really? Oh my! Jack hasn't mentioned that to me."

"I don't think Tyler has told many people. Uncle Fred might not even know," said Lisa, unlocking her sporty convertible.

"See you tomorrow. I can't wait to hear the latest Dobach Mechanical gossip!" smiled Angie.

As Lisa waved good-bye, she wondered if Tyler's potential departure would be a good or bad thing? How might it affect Jack and his opportunities? How would the employees view the rather sudden departure of three family members—all of them having been there for at least a decade? She started her car; her mind was churning with questions and possibilities.

Jack and Tom went to see Fred. Finding his office empty, they walked to the conference room. Casey and Catherine had the table covered in presentation materials as they worked on a proposal. Fred, Velma, and Larry were helping, too.

"Jack! Good, come in. We need to talk," Fred said. "Tom, would you excuse us? We need to discuss a private matter."

"Of course. I'll wait for you in your office, Jack." Tom departed.

"What's going on?" Jack inquired. "Did I miss a meeting?"

"Not at all, son. This is strictly impromptu. I wanted to talk to all of you. Now that we've got the bank off our backs, I think we've gotten our value out of Tom and we need to let him go. His advice seems to have taken a not-very-family-friendly turn. I was told that Tom instructed Tyler that this isn't a good place for him and he needed to find a job somewhere else!"

There was stunned silence. For a few long seconds, no one spoke.

Catherine broke the silence. "That doesn't sound like Tom; there must be a little more to the story, don't you think?"

"I don't know. All I know is, I went home walking on air yesterday only to be met by my wife in hysterics telling me about 'that damn consultant.' And that was the nicest thing she called him. I have to agree with Daphne. If Tom is so full of himself he thinks he can pick and choose which family members work here and which don't, he's crossed a line with me, and he needs to go!"

Larry, in his deep, gravelly voice, chimed in. "I agree with Catherine. Tom has too good a head on his shoulders to go off half-cocked like that. There must be more to this. And is Tyler leaving? This is news to me!"

"Well, I haven't spoken with him yet. He told Daphne he was taking a job in Georgia. That's the extent of what I know," said Fred.

"Shouldn't we—someone—speak with Tyler? Before we make any rash decisions, we ought to have good information," said Catherine.

"I'll talk to him," said Fred.

"Mind if I come?" asked Larry. "If he chooses to leave, that means we're going to be a project manager short, and with new work coming online, I don't want to get caught unawares."

"OK, let's figure out just what the hell is going on," Fred said, heading out the door with Larry at his side.

Catherine began packing up her materials. "Do you think Tom really did what Uncle Fred said?" asked Catherine.

"I hope not," Jack replied. "I think he's done a whale of a job so far. And I'm excited about the plans he has for using the new business plan as a management tool, rolling it out for the employees, and finding some top talent to replace departing staff. I think there's still a lot of work for him to do."

"If he did what Fred says, he needs to go," asserted Velma. "On the other hand, it really doesn't sound like him; I agree with you on that point, Catherine. I guess we'll know more before long. And I don't really care whether Tom stays or goes as long as you find a replacement for me and I can be out of here in a few months—that's the main thing on my mind. The retirement bug has bitten me, and I'm looking forward to spending time at the beach!"

XIII
July 2014

It looked like our productive association with Tom Hartwell might be a short one. Emotions were running high, and, while our business prospects were improving, the family seemed to be suffering.

Amos was in Fred's office complaining about Tom and his "overly complicated cash flow projections."

"It's all smoke and mirrors, if you ask me. And he's got Jack believing in it one hundred percent! Hiring that guy was a big mistake!" Amos fumed.

"You might be right, Amos," Fred replied in a weary voice as he rubbed his left arm. "Tom knocked a home run with the business plan. You've got to give him that. But this whole Tyler business—"

When Larry and Fred had gone in search of Tyler, he was out at a job site. Fred left word for him to notify him immediately upon his return. That was hours ago, and Fred was antsy and unable to concentrate. He didn't know what Tom was working on now or where he was; he didn't want any more interaction with the consultant until he knew the whole story.

Amos continued. "I was just rolling up my sleeves to get into the business plan when Tom came in and upset the whole applecart. I could've done it, and I wouldn't have needed so many people meeting so many times either. I could've done it on my own."

Larry had just walked in and overheard Amos's comment. He chuckled and said, "I think you might be missing the point, Amos. Creating a team to brainstorm and produce the meat of the plan has benefits far beyond the black-and-white document in this binder." Larry hefted the written plan from Fred's desk. "If you think this is the sole benefit of our business planning process, you're not looking at it right. For the first time, Dobach's owners and key managers—well, apparently not all—are definitively on the same sheet of music for who we are as a company and where we're going. And Tom's idea for packaging parts of this up and rolling it out for every single employee is brilliant! We're going to have everyone under this roof rolling in unison in the exact same direction! There's no telling what we can accomplish now that we've got a clear, common vision! And this planning process—not the document itself, but the process of all of us collaborating together on its creation—is where the value is."

"I think you're giving Tom way too much credit," Amos asserted.

Just then, Fred's phone rang. Tyler was back and on his way to see his father. "Would you excuse us, Amos?"

"Sure," Amos replied prissily.

Tyler entered.

"Your mother tells me you might be leaving us. What the hell's going on? You want to tell us what you're thinking?" Fred began.

"I probably should've told you before I said anything to Mom," stated Tyler. "That may not have been the smartest thing. Anyway, yes, I have a job offer from a company in Georgia, and I think I should take it."

"Did Tom put you up to this?" Fred demanded.

"Not at all! I told him…well, I told him how unhappy I am here." Tyler's lower lip began to tremble slightly. "I have always felt pressure to live up to Granddad's standards and yours and Larry's and now Jack's. And I never have felt respected by you, Dad, or anyone else here. I feel like a screw-up ninety-nine percent of the time." A tear slipped down Tyler's cheek. Fred was leaning back in his chair; his son had never said these things before. "Everyone knows I didn't finish college. They all know I had drug and alcohol issues and that I failed as a husband and maybe a father too. They all suspect the only reason I have a job at all is because I'm your son! And I don't want that anymore. Tom didn't recommend I leave, but he gave me good advice on the value of having alternatives. He helped me understand that it was up to me to either accept the Status Quo or look in a different direction. Almost as a lark, I began to shop around online to see what jobs were out there, and believe it or not, there are lots of opportunities for a project manager with my experience! The offer in Atlanta is for a lot more money. But the main attraction for me is—" Tyler began to cry in earnest now. "I'll be able to see what I can do on my own. I'll be able to be my own man. There won't be family business pressure to live up to—Granddad's legacy or anyone else's. I'll be free to either sink or swim on my own."

Fred's eyes were brimming with tears, too. "Son, you never said these things before. This is all so new. We can do things differently around here! We can give you a raise—"

"No, Dad. Don't you see this is a good thing for me? I need to try this. I need to know I can make it on my own, just Tyler, just me. No Leon, no Larry, no Jack. Just me. My mind is made up."

"You can't just pick up and leave, son! You'd be putting Larry and the rest of us in a hell of a lurch!"

Tyler looked at Larry, who met his gaze. "I'm sure Larry and the rest of the guys can take up the slack, can't you, Larry?"

Looking up at the ceiling, Larry replied thoughtfully, "I guess so. We'll need some help from you to understand where you are with your projects, but we've managed before when PMs have left. This is kind of different, but I'm sure we can come up with a way to keep the work moving properly."

"You have a son, Tyler!" Fred said indignantly. "What about that responsibility?"

"Phyllis has primary custody as you well know, Dad. And I wouldn't be moving to Antarctica. I'm not planning on running out on my duties as a father," Tyler asserted coolly.

"Your mother is furious!" Fred thundered. "I don't know what she'll do if you continue with this foolishness! Why you just settle down, tell us what changes we need to make, and quit putting us through all this drama?"

"Dad, don't you think I've thought of all these things and more?" Tyler pleaded. "I'm not stupid—in spite of what you seem to think sometimes. I know this change is going to have ripple effects in the family and business. It's a huge step for me. I've never tried to be one hundred percent on my own before. I have about a thousand fears and concerns, but this is the right thing for me at the right time in my life!"

"Come to your senses, Tyler!" Fred said angrily. "There's just no need for you to leave the family and the business, and move down to Georgia! It's out of the question!" Fred looked at Tyler as if this were the final word.

"I said it before, Dad, my mind is made up!" Tyler crossed his arms in defiance.

"This conversation ain't over—not by a long shot!" Fred asserted as he, too, crossed his arms.

Tyler stood up to leave. "I love you, Dad. Mom, too. I want you both to understand my decision." Tears began to well in Tyler's eyes again. "Arguing about it isn't going to make me change my mind, and it makes me feel worse. This is the right thing for me to do; I feel it in my bones!" With that, Tyler turned on his heel and departed.

Fred looked at Larry and shook his head sadly. "Kids!" Larry nodded slowly in understanding.

The next morning, the Strategic Planning Project Team was at it again. "Why are we having another meeting?" Amos inquired. "The bank has approved the plan. Isn't your work done here, Tom?"

"Well, I guess that's always up to you all. The minute I quit adding value to the family and business, I should go. But I think there's still plenty of work to do. First, we want to take selected parts of the business plan, package them in an informative and attractive way, and have the company leaders roll it out for the benefit of the employees. For example, look at one of the things my company does." Tom reached into his wallet and pulled out a laminated credit-card-size item. "This is something everyone in my firm gets. This wallet-size document has our mission, vision, and values on this side, and on the other side we spell out our top company priorities for the year. It's just one way we make sure that the business plan gets translated from a dusty, binder-size theoretical document into a practical business management tool. We communicate the plan to get buy-in, to forge a team instead of just having a bunch of people working randomly in pursuit of their own narrow interests. We want everyone to feel they are part of something bigger than themselves—a business family, if you will."

"Wow, Tom! Just talking about it has you all fired up," Casey laughed. "I guess if you can get that jazzed, we might be able to get our folks excited about our vision for Dobach Mechanical. I can tell you, I've been on both winning and losing teams in my day. One thing winning teams always had—and losing teams didn't—was commitment to one another as teammates. The military calls it 'unit cohesion.' Tom is right: the winning teams I was part of saw themselves as something more than just a collection of individuals. We had a purpose, a focus, and a vision of ourselves as champions. If we can bring that type of team culture to Dobach Mechanical, it will be a great thing!"

Catherine smiled radiantly and beamed approval at her father.

"I don't see how this is going to happen like magic," Amos intoned. "This kind of razzle-dazzle stuff might work well with college kids, but with grown-up construction workers it won't be so easy."

Jack spoke up. "We can do it! Casey's right, and I saw this myself when I visited public companies as an analyst. Some businesses had an 'all for one and one for all' culture you could practically feel. If a public company with 50,000 employees scattered all over the world can do it, why can't we do it with our 250?"

"I think we're bound to try it," said Larry. "I love the idea of using the business plan as a management and measurement tool. I think it will allow us, as we push our new action plans deeper and deeper into the company, to hold our people more accountable. We'll be able to see who's really contributing and who isn't, and we'll be able to get, as Tom says, 'the wrong people off the bus and the right people on.'"

"Excellent!" Tom said. "Jack, Catherine, and I will rough out the rollout and communication plan and schedule. Then we'll reconvene this group, make the necessary changes and improvements, and prep Fred, Velma, and Casey for their rollout presentations."

He continued. "The second initiative we need to get cracking on is developing your HR capabilities for attracting, vetting, hiring, training, and retaining new talent. We have to replace Velma and Tyler at the very least, and we might need to replace Addie, too. Getting warm bodies in those places in the organization isn't good enough. We need some seriously talented people to come in and help us energize our new cultural initiatives."

"Looks like I'm getting out at the right time!" joked Velma. "I don't know if I have what it takes to cut it around here anymore."

Everyone laughed.

Smiling, Tom said, "Well, there's plenty for us to do in the next few weeks. Let's get going!"

Fred and Larry were engrossed in a set of plans. Tyler tapped on Fred's door. "Come on in, son," Fred said. "Larry and I are going over some of your plans." He turned to Larry. "In spite of our advice and arguments, Tyler seems determined to leave us, Larry. I can't tell you we're thrilled about it, but Daphne and I have started to make peace with his decision. Tyler will be wrapping things up with us at the end of next week. That company in Atlanta is going to get a hell of a project manager!" Fred said with a wry smile.

Larry stood up and offered his hand. "Good luck to you, Tyler! I'm excited for you. We hate to lose you, but I'm impressed with your resolve and wish you the very best. You let me know if we can help you, and we will come running!"

"Thanks, Larry. That means a lot. You know how much I respect you; thanks for your support!"

"Let's take these plans down to my office and gather up a few others. We probably don't need to waste any more of Fred's time." Larry departed, his arms filled with plans.

"OK; I'll be right there, Larry." Tyler turned to his father. "I love you, Dad. I know you don't agree with me and that this hasn't been easy for you and Mom. But I'm glad you at least understand my decision." Fred stood, tears in his eyes, and gave Tyler a warm hug. Tyler couldn't remember the last time his dad had hugged him; it was a great feeling.

XIV
August 2014

Fred, Velma, Casey, and Tom were walking out of the bank having updated Barney and the bank's president on the past sixty days since the plan unveiling meeting in June. They also laid out the reporting format for our quarterly cash flow projections. The bankers were again most complimentary about the work Dobach Mechanical was doing, and the meeting lifted everyone's spirits.

"That went pretty damn well, Tom. You really speak the same language as those bankers. I thought they might try to kiss you square on the mouth before it was over!" Casey exclaimed.

"Thank you, Casey," Tom said, laughing. "I appreciate that. It does look like we're giving them what they want. More importantly, the changes we've made are bearing fruit. I think this is going to be a good year for profits."

"Since you're in town, do you want to come over for Tyler's going away party at my house tonight, Tom?" asked Fred.

"Thank you; I'd be delighted!" he replied. "How nice of you to ask!"

"He just wants you there for protection in case Daphne pulls a one-eighty at the thought of her baby moving eight hours away!" joked Casey.

"I'll wear body armor," Tom teased.

Daphne, Velma, Angie, and Lisa were doing some last-minute decorating. The family was excited for Tyler, and they wanted him to know how dear he was to them as he took off on a bold new course.

"It's been a crazy summer!" Lisa said enthusiastically. "Both Tyler and Addie are making huge changes. I think it's awesome how they've decided to take charge of their lives."

"I hope that's all the change we're going to have for a while!" stated Velma. "This excitement and drama is enough to last me a long time!"

The guests began to arrive. Casey and Amber made a beeline for the bar. Amber had on a bright-green scoop-neck party dress that emphasized her new curves. Velma and Daphne looked at each other, rolled their eyes, and chuckled. Addie made her entrance: she had changed her hair, lost a few pounds, and was wearing a colorful print dress instead of her old shapeless earth tones. She looked healthier, stronger, and more self-aware than in the past. Arthur strolled in looking like the stereotypical successful Southern lawyer. The G3 family members began to arrive in groups of twos and threes. Larry and Tom came in together. Everyone was in high spirits, and the drinks and conversation flowed freely.

Catherine came onto the pool deck, and everyone immediately looked in her direction. She usually wore little or no makeup, along with stylish but conservative business outfits, and pulled her hair back into a ponytail. Tonight, however, she wore a beautifully tailored black cocktail dress, diamond earrings on loan from her mother, tastefully applied makeup, high heels, and a swept-up hairstyle. She looked like she had stepped right off the pages of *Vogue*. Casey had never seen his daughter look so beautiful. "You look great, sweetheart! It's hard to believe someone with your looks has such a big brain. You're the total package!"

"Thank you, Dad!"

About fifteen minutes after everyone else had arrived, Tyler made his entrance. He was wearing khaki trousers and a white button-down shirt. Fred couldn't remember the last time he'd seen Tyler wear a navy blazer; he hadn't even known he owned a sport coat. Tyler worked the group like a politician. With his new, much shorter haircut and fresh attire, he looked like he was ready to take on the world. This was a Tyler the family had rarely seen. He tapped his water glass with a spoon. "Thank you all for coming! I really appreciate Mom and Dad going to the trouble and expense—"

"Don't worry!" interrupted Casey. "He'll find a way to expense it to the company!"

The crowd erupted in laughter.

"As I was saying, it's a great honor for me for you all to come and show your support. I'm genuinely touched. And I hope I'll make you all proud in my new job."

"You'll be the best project manager in Georgia!" exclaimed Larry. "After all, I trained you myself!"

Everyone smiled and nodded approval they raised their glasses in toast to Tyler.

A while later, Jack, Larry, and Tom were in deep conversation. Fred and Casey wandered over. "What are you three conspiring about?" Casey asked in a good-natured way. No one answered. "Is something going on? What's up?" Fred asked, a note of concern entering his voice.

"Maybe it's not the right time or place, Fred, but we were talking shop over here," Tom said. "Let me just run something up the flagpole with you, and then we'll let you get back to the party. With Velma and Addie's departures, the admin and finance department has lost one-third of its staff. We're enjoying the short-term salary savings, but there could be some long-term consequences. After all, there's still plenty of work to do. And, to be blunt about it, we were discussing another personnel change in finance."

As Fred exhaled cigarette smoke, he said, "Get to the point, Tom. Daphne is giving me dirty looks over here."

"OK, here goes. We want to let Amos go and install Jack as the new controller. That's the heart of it."

"What! Amos has been with us for a quarter century! Except for this little mix-up with my damn fool brother"—Casey looked at his shoes, his lips pressed tightly together—"he's been as solid an employee as you could ask for!" Fred practically shouted.

"Fred," Larry said softly, "This is not the time or place. Let's talk more at the office next week."

"All right," Fred said huffily. "But you three don't need to be cooking up conspiracies about who we should fire! Put the business talk away for a while and enjoy the party."

Fred turned on his heel and left. The festivities carried on as the clock approached midnight.

Fred, Daphne, Jack, and Angie were cleaning up around the pool, gathering up wineglasses, and bagging trash. The party been great fun and a huge success.

"That was lovely! I hope Tyler knows how much we're going to miss him!" Daphne said.

"Come on, Mom," Jack teased. "You've already booked monthly flights to Atlanta, haven't you?"

"Well, someone has to make sure Tyler's apartment is furnished and he has groceries. That boy would forget his head if it weren't screwed on," said Daphne lightheartedly.

"I must've had one too many," Fred said, holding on to the back of a pool chair for support. "I feel awful!"

"Sit down, Fred," commanded Angie. "Your color doesn't look good."

"I'm OK," Fred assured everyone. "I'm just too damn old to stay up this late on a Friday night. Let's get these dishes inside, and I'll turn in."

The group continued to tidy up and made their way to the kitchen. Daphne exclaimed "Fred! You don't look right! Now that I see you in the light, you're as pale as a ghost!"

Fred rotated his left arm. "I must've pulled a muscle or something lifting those heavy trash bags."

"Are you saying you have pain in your left arm, Fred?" asked Angie in an eerily calm voice.

"Yes, a little, but I'm sure it's nothing a good night's sleep won't cure. Is it hot in here to you? I'm sweating like a pig!" Angie grabbed her cell phone and immediately dialed 911.

"What are you doing?" Daphne said shrilly. "He said he'd be OK."

"This is nothing to take lightly!" Jack said. "Angie is calling the paramedics, and Dad needs to get checked out. If it's nothing, we'll all be relieved. If it's a heart issue, you need to know that, and every minute may count!"

"This is no way to start off a weekend," Fred said dryly.

XV
August 2014

It seemed like our family had spent more time together at hospitals this year than we had in all others combined. At the hospital, the group tittered with conversation about Fred and his condition.

"That was a wonderful party. I sure didn't expect to follow it up with more time spent here," sighed Velma.

"You said it, sis," Casey responded. "Old Fred looked as happy as a clam the last few days. He was so proud of Tyler setting off in a new, hopefully successful direction. It just ain't right that he gets sick."

"All those years of smoking and drinking take a toll," commented Amber. All eyes snapped in her direction. "What? It's the truth; everyone knows smoking is bad for you."

"Amber, honey, why don't you scoot off and try to round us up a cup of coffee?" Casey cooed.

"Why are you always acting like you're embarrassed to have me around? I'm your wife! Why won't you stand by me? I'm only saying what everyone knows!" Casey escorted Amber away by the elbow. They were talking animatedly to each other.

"I'm sorry, Daphne," said Velma. "That horrible little woman says the rudest things sometimes."

"She didn't mean any harm," replied Daphne. "And she's right: Fred doesn't take the greatest care of himself. We can both do better. Here's the doctor!"

"Mrs. Dobach. You did the right thing bringing your husband in. Early indications are that he did have a mild heart attack. We're running more tests now; then we'll admit Fred to the hospital. We'll keep him here at least a day or two. You might want to send someone home to get Mr. Dobach's toiletries and other things. He's stable now, and we don't think there's much damage to the heart muscle. Chances are he'll be home in a few days and back to work soon after. But he's going to have to make some lifestyle changes."

"Thank you, Doctor. For all my worrying, I guess it could've been worse."

"Yes, ma'am, it could've been much worse. Do you have any questions?"

"When can I see Fred?"

"He's having some tests now. As soon as they're done, we can take you back to be with him."

"Thank you."

The doctor turned and reentered the medical facility.

"Mom, Angie and I can go pack up some things for Dad," Jack offered. "What about you? Are you going to stay here?"

"I guess so. Better pack some things for me, too."

"Will do. Aunt Velma, do you need anything?" Jack inquired.

"No, Jack, thank you. We'll be going once we see Fred. Oh, Reverend Henley. How nice of you to come." Velma and the others shook hands and exchanged hugs with their minister as Jack and Angie left the hospital.

At Dobach Mechanical, Catherine hung up the phone and sprang from her chair. She ran into the hallway, head whipping back and forth, looking as if she'd burst if she didn't find someone with whom to share her news. Hearing Larry's gruff voice, she took off toward his office. "We got it! We got it!" she shouted.

"Got what? You look like you're going to bust a gut, girl! Slow down!"

"I just got off the phone with the folks at Hibberts Development. You know that big project Dad and I presented on last week? We got it! This is our biggest project ever—almost $25 million! I wish Dad and Uncle Fred were here!"

"That's great, Catherine!" Larry stood, and they exchanged high fives. "All that preconstruction work we did paid off in a big way! Congratulations!"

Heath heard all the commotion. "Did we get it?" he asked.

"We did! We did!" Catherine exclaimed gleefully.

"I love it when a plan comes together!" Larry exclaimed. "This thing ought to be a home run for us. It's pretty complex, but our margins are excellent! Plus, we'll be partnering with owners and GCs we've worked with successfully before. The business development team"—Larry winked at Catherine—"ought to get a nice steak dinner compliments of Dobach Mechanical."

"Considering Fred's condition, maybe you should stick with fish!" Heath joked.

"This news ought to perk Fred up a little." Larry grabbed some papers from his desk and began scribbling furiously. "Our backlog now is…$70 million or close to it. That's as high as it's ever been, Catherine! You and Casey have been doing great promoting us and securing new work."

"Thank you. Dad has been a new man since his 'incident.' He was so embarrassed. It's ironic that something like that would motivate him so."

"You've got to give yourself some credit, too, Catherine," interjected Larry. "You've been a real asset!" Catherine look sheepishly at the floor, her cheeks flushing a bit at the compliment.

"Who knows what will spur someone to a better performance?" Heath opined. "Maybe we should find a way to embarrass all of us if the payoff is going to be like this!"

Larry and Catherine laughed. Larry's phone rang, signaling an end to the brief celebration. "OK, everyone, back to work!" Larry bellowed as he took the call.

A week later, Tom Hartwell stopped by Fred's house for a visit. There were flowers still about, and Daphne was struggling with where to store all the food friends and neighbors had delivered. She greeted Tom coolly; she still felt ambivalent toward him, assuming he'd had a hand in her favorite son's relocation.

Tom found Fred in a recliner in the den watching Sports Center. "Fred! It's good to see you out of the hospital!"

"Hello, Tom. I'm glad to be home. I'm sick of needles, nurses, and tests."

"How do you feel? What's your prognosis?"

"The doctors say there's some damage to my heart. One thing's for sure: I won't be smoking anymore! And I have to go exercise every morning; that's taking some getting used to. I tell you, Tom, this has put a real scare into me. Dad was eighty-one when he died. I'm only seventeen years away from that. That's barely the blink of an eye! Death and taxes, you know—"

Fred continued in a low tone. "When you have a scare like this, it really makes you reflect on things—how you live, how you treat yourself and other people. Tom, I really don't see myself going back to work full-time. Maybe I've been on cruise control for a while anyway. Maybe that's how we got into such a vulnerable position in the spring; no one was truly on the lookout for the kind of threats that almost took us down. I was too set in my ways, too cocky, too overconfident, and too complacent that just because we'd been so successful for so long, everything would magically take care of itself without any real intervention on my part."

"You're being pretty hard on yourself, Fred. Lots of family businesses have had to deal with upheaval since the Great Recession changed the way we do business. But this decision about you not coming in full-time anymore...that's pretty sudden. Have you guys as family business owners given any time and attention to management succession planning?" asked Tom gently.

"Yes. We all have wills and trusts—Arthur helped us get a top estate man for all that."

"That's not what I mean," Tom explained. "That's ownership succession—what I call 'Drop Dead Planning.' You're not gone yet, and if I know you, you have a lot of years left. And even if you, Velma, or Casey got struck by lightning, the odds of something happening to all three of you at the same time is astronomical. No, I mean *management succession planning.* Who would take over your duties as president? What are the requirements of the position, especially now that Dobach Mechanical looks poised for growth in the next few years? Who and what resources will you need to run a different company in a different future? Those are the questions I'm asking."

"Well, Jack is certainly capable. But he's only been back a few years. And I guess we've done a terrible job grooming him. Until recently, since you came aboard, we really hadn't challenged Jack at all. Could he take my place?" asked Fred.

"He certainly has the talent and intelligence. But is he ready to be the top guy? Is he ready to make decisions that affect the futures of 250 employees and their families? I'm not sure; it may be too early yet," Tom mused. "Besides, we have tentatively slated Jack as Amos's replacement as controller and eventually CFO. Amos is sixty-six and isn't exactly enthusiastic about some of the changes we're making."

"Don't kick Amos out the door just yet, Tom! He's been loyal and faithful to us for twenty-five years. But we do need to challenge Jack more." Fred thought for a moment. "Hey! What about you as my replacement? You've done a great job getting us going in a better direction. Everyone's excited about our new business plan, the employees are engaged, and our prospects look bright. Why can't you be the next president until Jack is ready?"

"That's awfully flattering, Fred, but I'm not your man. I'm done running companies. I prefer the shorter-term consulting assignments now. They're more fun and a heck of a lot less pressure," Tom smiled. "No, I think we need to do a comprehensive search just like we were planning to do for Velma's replacement. The SPPT is meeting again tomorrow. Let's start off with you telling the group what you're thinking and gauge their reaction. We might need to expand our executive search. What do you think?"

"I don't want to paint myself into a corner, but I really don't see myself coming back full-time and leading all these changes. We need somebody younger with more energy and passion. Forty years in the mechanical contracting businesses is enough to wear a fellow down!"

Tom replied, "Forty years doing anything is a long time. You can run your idea by the team tomorrow, and we'll determine next steps from there."

XVI

September 2014

So far, Fred had only discussed his desire to slow down with Tom. Today he would outline his intentions with the rest of our employee family. How would they react? And what changes would this new turn of events necessitate?

Fred, Velma, Casey, Jack, Catherine, Heath, Larry, and Amos—the SPPT—were in session. There was the usual banter prior to getting under way.

Casey looked across the table at Amos. "Windy outside this morning, Amos? I see a little more scalp than usual."

Amos's hair, normally painstakingly arranged and sprayed, was all over the place. Amos flushed as his hands flew to his head for some last-minute rearranging.

"Leave him alone, Casey! We've got a lot to do today, so let's get down to it," snapped Fred. "First, let me just say how grateful I feel for everyone's kindness. I really appreciate you all rallying around. And I know Daphne feels the same. The doctors would probably skin me if they knew I was back in the office already, but I've got something important to tell everyone. One thing about having a heart attack: it will focus your mind!"

He continued. "I've been at it for a good long time. We've all been at it a long time, if you think about Velma, Casey, and Larry, too. And I'm not sure—given all the changes we're making—that

I'm the right guy to stay on as president of the company. I don't have the passion and energy I used to, and I think Dobach Mechanical could use a guy who is better trained to run such a big and growing enterprise."

"Don't be so hasty, Fred!" said Velma. "You've done an excellent job, and we need you! You'll be back to full strength soon!"

"That's right, brother!" Casey asserted. "Replacing Dad was a tall order, and we've done OK on your watch. I think you're making a decision much too soon. Don't be rash; give yourself more time!"

"OK, OK! I'm not exactly running for the door, and I appreciate the kind comments and support, but I'm serious. Velma has decided she wants out; we called this meeting to talk about how we'd replace Velma and Addie in admin/finance. And I think we need to seriously consider looking for a crackerjack young executive to take my place as president. I'll stick around until we can get someone else on board. I'm even willing to stay beyond that as a consultant or mentor as long as I can be productive. My only point is that we need somebody who can devote serious time and energy to helping us get to the next level and fulfill our potential."

Larry spoke up. "Well, this being a family business and all, the logical sequence says Jack would be the next president. You replaced your dad; why can't Jack replace you?"

"Thanks for the vote of confidence, Larry," said Jack. "But I've only been back a few years, and frankly, I don't really know the full scope and breadth of what we do around here. I'm more comfortable with finance and administration than the actual work of mechanical contracting. I'd like to think that I could grow into the job eventually, but Dobach Mechanical, with all the great things we have going on, probably needs someone more experienced than a thirty-one-year-old who has spent half his career working in a completely unrelated industry."

"I appreciate you saying that, son," Fred said softly. "You'd be a helluva president, I'm sure of it. But I have to confess, Tom and I were thinking along those same lines. My reaction was, bluntly, to offer Tom the job." Amos turned a ghastly shade of white. "But he turned me down cold." Tom smiled and nodded in assent. "Our consultant here thinks we can find the right person by conducting a nationwide job search."

"We've never had a president who wasn't a family member," Amos began. "I think Leon would turn over in his grave if he knew you all were thinking of going outside the family for the next one! In addition, I don't see how an outsider could come in here and understand how we do things. It would take years for someone to get up to speed. By the time you train up this outsider, Jack could've been trained just as easily. Plus, what will we have to pay an outsider? Fred gets a pretty good paycheck, but I bet an outsider would cost us a whole lot more. No, I think it's a mistake to try to find some superstar from California, or Florida, or God only knows where, and then fly him in here, have him set up shop, and expect him to run the company with any degree of success. I just don't see how that plan can work!"

"Way to try and throw cold water on things as usual, Amos!" Casey needled. "If big companies with billions of dollars of revenue and tens of thousands of employees scattered all over the world can replace a CEO every few years, it stands to reason that we can replace a president once a generation or so. If he is bound and determined to step away—and I'm on record as saying he should wait to make that call—Fred is right. The three of us have been leading this company for a long time, and while we've had some successes, we've made some pretty big blunders, too. Maybe it is time to look outside for some talent who can build on all the positives we've put together over the course of the spring and summer. And by the time that person is ready to move on, Catherine or Jack might be in a good position to take over."

"You're not going to find a CEO-caliber person by placing an ad in the paper," Amos huffed. "And headhunters cost a fortune!"

Tom replied, "That's true, Amos. I'm thinking what we really need is a hiring program on steroids. Forget the local paper and the ways you have traditionally tried to get new people. This needs to be different; we need to pull out all the stops to give ourselves the best possible chance of finding just the right candidate who shares our company and family values, and who can lead us to a higher plane. I envision a nationwide search using the latest hiring best practices including psychometric testing, practical assignments, and group interviewing techniques. I think we should be very deliberate, and the process should last somewhere between seventy-five and a hundred days. If we don't think we have attracted world-class talent in the first batch of candidates, we'll go back and repeat the process until we find the right person. It would be my goal to get at least one hundred applicants; I bet for a company like this in your city we could generate over three hundred."

"Three hundred applications! That's absurd!" Amos blurted. "We wouldn't know what to do with that many. All other work around here would have to stop while we sorted through them!"

Tom made a placating motion with his hands. "Don't worry. There will be plenty of time for everyone to get their normal jobs done. And we'll do this project ourselves; there won't be any headhunters involved. There will be some costs in advertising, recruiting, psychometric tests, flying candidates in for interviews, etc., but they won't be great, and it will be well worth it when we find the perfect person."

"This sounds like a big and important project, Tom. Are you sure this is something we can handle by ourselves? We've never done hiring like this," said Velma.

"Velma," Jack stated, "this is the kind of process I went through before I went to work on Wall Street. They had a bunch of industrial psychologists help them design the program to make sure they got not only very smart people but also ones who shared the values of the other people in the firm. If they can do it, we can, too. With Tom's help, we have the capability to do this. And we can apply this more rigorous hiring standard up and down the company. We need to do this type of search to find your replacement anyway, so it makes sense to use a modern best-practices methodology as we look for two new executives instead of just one."

"I like it, too," said Larry. "At my age and stage, I wouldn't want to work for just any young buck. I want to make sure that if I'm going to throw in with a president not named Fred Dobach that he's the kind of guy I can really respect and get behind. It sounds like Tom has done this before and has a good process for helping us make sure we hit the bull's-eye."

"What's the first thing we need to do, Tom?" asked Fred.

"I'll put together an action plan for everyone to review and to keep us all on the same page. Off the top of my head, I think the first thing we need to do is invest about thirty minutes in brain-storming about what the 'perfect candidate' is like."

Catherine spoke up. "That sounds like an interesting exercise, but how does it help us find the right person?"

"Great question. The reason we want to do this is to develop some cohesion on the kind of person who represents that perfect candidate. Since this discussion will never leave this room, we can go in any direction we want. We could speculate that our top candidate will be a certain gender, a certain race, a certain religion, a certain height, a certain weight, have certain professional designations, anything we want. The main thing is that we have a healthy discussion and decide which attributes are important and which aren't. Then once we have some general agreement on what the perfect candidate is like, we'll hold applicants up to this template and see how they measure up. If we see somebody who scores well, for example, on nineteen out of twenty-one items, we'll know that person is probably better suited for the job than someone who only scores on nine of twenty-one."

"That makes sense," said Catherine. "I don't know if that's been a part of our hiring system in the past—"

"It hasn't been," Amos interrupted.

"But I do like the idea of pre-agreeing on what the top candidates should have in the way of qualifications and attributes."

"So let's get started." Tom pulled out his ubiquitous easel pad and began to adhere pages to the wall. "Let's have fun with this; we can go in a hundred different directions. For example, does the person's gender matter?" He looked around the room as everyone shook their heads in the negative. "Good! We're off and running? What about race. Do we care about that?" Again, all heads shook in the negative. "OK. What attributes *do* we care about?"

"All other things being equal, we're a Christian family, and Dad always wanted us to run the company based on Christian values. I hope we've been true to his vision for the most part!" Fred noticed Velma nodding in agreement. "For that reason, I would prefer someone who shares our Christian values."

"I agree," said Velma and Larry almost simultaneously.

"I'm not sure what percentage of our workforce holds themselves out as Christian, but I would be surprised if it wasn't a sizeable majority," Casey added.

Amos offered, "Aren't we getting into some discrimination and hiring violation issues here?"

"I don't think so," said Tom. "Remember, this exercise is only to get us all on the same page and won't leave this room. Besides, if a terrific candidate walked in the door who didn't happen to be a Christian, we wouldn't automatically boot him from consideration, would we?"

"Of course we wouldn't!" said Heath.

"What else is important then?" asked Tom.

"I have a whole list of things," offered Catherine. "For example, education needs to be on the list along with relevant work experience. We don't want to try, in my opinion, a person who's never run a contracting firm before. We want someone who's had success leading and managing people, and building cohesive teams. Furthermore, I think we need someone who's run a company much larger than ours. It would be great to get someone who has experience being in the place we want to go. That kind of experience would be invaluable in helping us avoid pitfalls that have plagued other companies as they've grown bigger and more complex."

There were murmurs of agreement around the table.

"Well done, Catherine. This is the kind of stuff we need!" Tom said.

Jack stated, "Environmentally sensitive construction experience and certifications ought to be on the list. That's one thing that can help set us apart from the competition."

Heads nodded in agreement.

The group continued for about twenty more minutes. At the end of the session, they had come up with a list of twenty-three attributes they thought would be important as they shopped for Fred's replacement. Then they invested another thirty minutes discussing what the next vice president of admin/finance would look like.

"The next exercise this group needs to undertake is to develop a comprehensive job description," Tom instructed.

"A job description!" whined Amos. "Why would you need a job description for the president of a company? Fred never had one, and Leon surely never did!"

"You're right again, Amos," Tom said. "This is a little bit different, however. In this case, a candidate is going to want to know exactly what's expected of her and how she's going to be held accountable by the owners of this business. It's not going to be sufficient to let an incoming president define her role any way she sees fit. She may expand or amend the role over time, and if that happens, we'll edit the job description. However, in the beginning, it's the owners and senior managers of this company who have to create expectations for the new president's responsibilities and hold her accountable."

"Absolutely right!" exclaimed Jack. "This is another place where we all have to be on the same page. It wouldn't be fair to a new, nonfamily president to start with anything other than crystal-clear expectations."

Velma said, "We've never had a job description for any of the senior officers in the company. This is new, too. Have you got a rabbit you can pull out of your hat on this one, Tom?"

"Sure do. I'll gather some we've used successfully in the past, and we'll customize new ones for your replacement as well as Fred's. And once we have the job descriptions all mapped out, we'll start placing ads on job boards. This process will take a little while, but we already have taken the first few steps and we're under way. Keep your eyes on your e-mails. I'll have the action plan in everyone's hands by tomorrow, and we can flesh out the job description more the next time we get together." Tom looked at his watch. "It's been a busy day, everyone. Maybe we should stop now."

The people around the conference table pushed their chairs back, stretched, and gathered up their materials. Amos fell in with Fred as they walked down the hall.

"Fred, I think you're making a mistake. This company and family have been dependent on you for so long. I just don't see how getting an outsider is going to work. And all this elaborate hiring with 'the perfect candidate' and an action plan and a job description...we never needed that stuff before!"

Fred laid his arm around Amos's bony, narrow shoulders. "Amos, I know all this makes you uncomfortable. It's not easy for any of us. But you saw the group—Catherine, Jack, even Larry. They're excited about the progress we've made and the potential we have. I know it's hard on you, old buddy, but keep your chin up. Now that we have this momentum, we don't want to lose it! And I've had a real change of heart—no pun intended! A heart attack will make you rethink things."

Amos mumbled, "I guess you're right."

XVII

September 2014

If someone had told us a year ago that both Fred and Velma would be leaving the company within a few months of each other, there would've been blind panic. Now, since we'd built up our change management muscles, their pending departures didn't seem like such a threat. And we were excited about Tom's process for getting some superstar talent on board. Now we needed to add some of the same planning tools we had utilized for the business and adapt them for the family.

Velma, Daphne, Catherine, Lisa, Heath, and Angie were settling in for a meeting with Tom Hartwell. Velma started things off. "Thanks for coming everyone. You know, I've been recommending for some time that we start a family council and establish regular, recurring meetings. I have friends with family businesses who have put this idea in place for their families, and they love it. I think Allen's family may have done something like this, too, right, Lisa?"

"That's right. Allen's family started meeting regularly a couple years ago, at Tom's suggestion, and they seem to get quite a kick out of their family council. They discuss the family business a little bit, but the meetings are really about strengthening and preserving the bonds of family—the things that make Allen's family unique. I've been to almost all of them; they made the decision to have the in-laws involved from the very beginning, and obviously, I'm happy they did. That's something we should talk about, too. It would be a real mistake to kick off any kind of family governance body without having spouses involved. Ultimately, we'll want to get...oh, I'm sorry, I don't mean to hijack your meeting, Velma. I'm talking way too much."

"Not all, Lisa. That's one of the reasons I wanted you here. You're the only one of us with direct experience with family council meetings—besides Tom, of course."

Daphne spoke up. "I think I get a sense of where you're going with this, Velma, but maybe you could tell us more about what a family council is supposed to do."

Velma replied, "I'll give you a few of the ideas that I've had about what the family council might do, and I've also asked Tom to help me flesh out some of the things he's experienced that work really well for others. My main concern is that as Addie and I—Fred, too, now—get away from the day-to-day of the family business, we'll lose contact with not only the business but the people side of things as well. I don't know if Fred has said anything similar to you, Daphne"—Daphne shook her head—"but I think we can work on communication quite a bit. Addie's oldest daughter, Sullivan, is seventeen years old now; she's practically grown. There might be some questions that these young people have as they come along about the history of the family, the history of the business, and so on. We also need to be thinking about putting rules in place for how family members can come into the business as employees. There's about sixteen years difference between the oldest G4 member and the youngest; that could lead to a lot of confusion about who gets what role, who gets what kind of job, who has authority over someone else, who gets paid what, and that sort of thing. When siblings or cousins in a family business begin carving out turf for their kids and trying to protect them, things can get awfully messy really fast.

"I also see that we have a need to make sure that those of us who aren't or soon won't be in the business anymore have some insight into how the construction and real estate companies are doing. It's going to be strange and uncomfortable, I think, for me and Addie who have been working with the numbers for so long to suddenly not be in the loop. I want to be kept informed—not that I want to get back into a decision-making role or anything, but I want to know the condition of our family business assets. After putting in over thirty years, not having any insight into the company's health and well-being might be too much for me to bear."

Tom inserted, "One of the most important things I think you could undertake as a family council is to begin to put together a history of the business. Two-thirds of G2 might be rather unexpectedly and suddenly retiring in the next few months, and Leon's been gone for a few years. I'd love to see you guys put together recollections, old photographs, anything you can find that belonged to Leon and Myra in the early days. We don't have to write a five-hundred-page potboiler about the Dobach family, but getting some of the family and business history documented would be a great blessing for not just you all, but especially for G3 and G4. Catherine here, for example, was only a child when Leon passed. I bet there's an immense amount of information that you have between your ears and tucked into the back of the attic that she and the other G3 members would love to know about."

"That does sound like fun!" said Daphne. "Fred has a bunch of old scrapbooks on the bookshelves in his study. I bet he's got tons of pictures from the early days of the business. And I know Myra has lots of old Polaroids from when Fred, Velma, and Casey were little."

Angie nodded with interest.

"I bet Allen's family would be happy to share what they've put together as a model for us to use as we build a history of the Dobach family," Lisa said cheerily.

"I bet they would, too," Tom agreed.

"Are the six of us going to be the…for lack of a better term, the family council committee?" asked Catherine.

"What do you all think?" asked Tom. "Are you willing to volunteer?"

"I'm not sure how much help I'd be," said Heath, "but I'd be happy to serve on the committee. It sounds like fun, and I have to admit that, as an in-law, it would be good to know more about the family business where I've been working the past six years."

Daphne and others quickly and enthusiastically stated that they, too, would be pleased to be on the committee.

"Excellent!" said Tom with a grin. "Thanks to all of you! I think that this will be a rewarding experience. There are three more things I think we should put on the agenda for the first meeting. The first thing is, I'd like to do is some personality assessments and prepare some basic education in order to help everyone understand everyone else in the group a little bit better. We'll use the Myers-Briggs Type Indicator and some other instruments. The second thing we'll need to add to the mix is to begin to formulate and document your family values, vision, and mission. We probably won't be able to complete this at the first family council meeting, and it might even take two or three meetings to get things just so, but mission, vison, and values are important foundational steps in getting the family council kicked off in a positive way. Third, we want to plan some family fun time, time that's not too structured and allows for the family to interact in a relaxed, comfortable way."

Lisa raised her hand, practically vibrating with energy. "I want to work on that! That's right up my alley!"

Smiling broadly at Lisa, Catherine said, "I'll work with you on the fun stuff, Lisa. You've got me excited about it, too."

"Very good, very good," Tom said. "Velma, thank you so much for getting this moving. Did you think it was going to be this easy?"

"I didn't. I thought there would be more pushback and less enthusiasm. I've been talking about a family council for some time, but for whatever reason, there wasn't much enthusiasm for the idea until now. Maybe you have something to do with that, Tom."

"I'm not too sure about that!" said Tom smiling. "There are two more serious things that we need to discuss. Those are the two budgets: the time budget and the money budget. The time budget has two components. First, how much time do we need to plan to put together the first meeting, and what duration meeting should we shoot for? We want to make sure the first one is a resounding success; if it's not, it will make it harder to engender enthusiasm for others down the road. And the money budget: when we put together the business plan for Dobach Mechanical, we didn't set aside any budget dollars to fund a family council. Depending on where you want to meet and what time of year, getting the family together could add up to quite a few dollars."

"Let me work on that, Tom!" Velma asserted. "Since this is kind of my idea, I ought to be the one who tries to find the money. Between the mechanical and the two real estate companies, we ought to be able to find enough money to do something reasonably nice this first year, and then we can build family council money into future business budgets going forward."

"Go get 'em, Velma!" shouted Daphne gleefully. "I can guarantee that Fred's going to be open to this idea, and I'm sure Casey will be, too. Don't you think so, girls?"

Catherine and Lisa both nodded.

"OK. Everyone's assignment is to begin seriously thinking about a couple days we can carve out of the calendar before the end of the year to have our inaugural family council meeting. I'll send an e-mail to everyone in the group to suggest a few possible dates, and I'll need you guys to be the cheerleaders for this effort," Tom concluded.

As the meeting began to break up, Velma sought out Daphne. "I'm going to see Mom at Forest Glen. If you don't have anything planned this afternoon, would you like to go with me? I'm going to swing by and pick up Addie, and maybe we could have a late lunch."

"That sounds fine. It's been a few weeks since I've seen Myra, and it will be nice to catch up with Addie. Shall we go?"

The ladies headed for the parking lot.

Seeing Myra was always a bittersweet experience. Myra, and all the residents at Forest Glen, were thrilled to have visitors and were gracious with their welcome and hospitality. On the other hand, it was difficult to see Myra struggling with her physical infirmities and accelerating mental decline. Velma knocked on Myra's door. They could hear her television clearly; the volume was turned way up. Velma pulled out her cell phone. "She can't hear us knocking for all that noise. But somehow she always hears her phone ring."

"Mom? It's Velma. Velma! We are at your door. Can you turn down your television and let us in?"

A minute later, they heard the dead bolt flip open.

"Velma! Daphne! And who's this nice lady?"

"Mom, this is your granddaughter Addie—you remember Addie."

"Addie! Please forgive me. Of course I remember my little grand-daughter. You look different. Have you lost weight?"

"Grandmother, I've lost almost twenty pounds! Thank you for noticing. You look great! Have you had your hair done?"

"I got my hair set just today. How does it look?"

"You look lovely!" Addie beamed, giving her grandmother a squeeze. "What were you watching on TV?"

"It's that handsome young minister from Texas. I just love watching him and his wife, too! In fact, I've been thinking about sending him some money. Velma, I still have some money of my own, don't I?"

"Yes you do, Mom."

"I'd like to send that young man $100,000. Can you write out the check for me to sign, Velma?"

"Myra, are you sure? Think about it: $100,000 is an awful lot of money to send to a preacher you never even met!" Daphne stated emphatically.

"I am sure!" insisted Myra. "I've been watching him for months and months. He's so handsome and enthusiastic. Now where's my checkbook?"

"Mom, don't you go off writing any checks like that! You don't even have $100,000 in a checking account. You could get in big trouble!" Velma asserted.

"Do I have $100,000 in any sort of account?" asked Myra.

"I think you're missing the point," Daphne said softly. "It's not whether or not you have the money; it's whether it would be appropriate to send so much of it off to this man in Texas. This is the kind of thing you really need to think and be sure about. You should let Fred and Velma advise you. You know Mrs. Webster and Mrs. Harrison from church—you remember them, right? They were both taken to the cleaners: one by an investment con man and one by a television preacher just like your man."

"He's not a con man! How dare you say that! That young man is as fine as any who's ever come along! I know if Leon were alive, he'd agree with me one hundred percent that we ought to send a donation right away!"

"Are you talking about my father Leon? Mom, you know how tight Dad was! He was pretty generous with our church and the Salvation Army, but he'd never in a million years agree to send even a fraction of $100,000 to someone he didn't even know!"

"I knew him better than you! I was married to the man, you know!"

Velma, Addie, and Daphne exchanged concerned glances. "Mom, maybe we could talk about this some other time. Would you like to join us for a late lunch? It's a pretty day outside; it might be fun for you to get out for little while."

"You won't let me send money to this man who needs it, but I bet you'll let me pay for lunch, won't you?" groused Myra.

"Maybe you'd better let me get lunch today, Mom," sighed Velma.

XVIII
October 2014

The SPPT was hard at work on its new assignment. Once Velma had decided she wanted to retire, a pressing HR challenge materialized. After Fred's heart attack and his subsequent announcement, the challenge became much broader, and it felt more intense. Contemplating hiring the first nonfamily president in Dobach Mechanical's history put a great deal of pressure on our group.

Tom passed out his action plan and kicked off the discussion. "Take a look at this, everyone." he said. "This is the action plan we'll use for finding both Fred and Velma's replacements—subject to your edits and approval, of course."

They studied the handout.

"There are six priority objectives and a little over thirty specific tasks. It looks a little bit involved and may be intimidating, but we want to make sure we capture every discrete step in the process of recruiting, screening, interviewing, assessing, and hiring the new executives. Furthermore, once we've been through this process at the executive hiring level, you can adapt it for hiring at any level of your organization. It should really professionalize how you do your staffing and allow you to increase the quality of the people you hire across the board. In effect, you'll be trained on this process as we try to find world-class replacements for Fred and Velma."

Casey gave a long whistle. "This is involved, Tom. Maybe too involved. It kind of has me on my heels a little bit."

Amos chipped in, "It's way too complicated, in my opinion. And a $3,500 budget? What's that all about?"

"The budget is to cover the costs of airline travel for any candidates who might need to come in for interviews, as well as overnight lodging, rental cars, and the cost of the psychometric evaluation tools. But, now that I think of it, that budget might be a little bit low given the fact we're looking for two new executives instead of one. Let's revise that number upward to $6,500."

Amos shook his head sadly.

Catherine had been concentrating intently. She said, "It looks very well thought out to me. But the devil is in the details. We need to flesh out our 'perfect candidate' profile and really dig into the job descriptions. Only after we've done those things can we kick off a formal search process, so we need to go deeper there."

Jack and Larry nodded their heads.

"Good," said Tom as he passed out another sheet of paper. "Here's the perfect candidate profile we began working on last time. Let's see how we can improve it."

"This may seem a little odd coming from me," said Velma, "but I'd like to go back to gender. I know we said it doesn't make any difference whether it's a man or woman who's the next president of the company or who replaces me, but I'm starting to wonder if we should revisit that. Construction is still such a man's world; I wonder if we'll get any quality female applicants. Should we just go ahead and assume we're going to end up with a man?"

Jack inquired, "Won't the applications themselves answer that question for us? In other words, if we get, as Tom suggested, one hundred applicants and only ten of them are from men, the odds will certainly favor hiring a female. On the other hand, if the numbers are reversed, we'll have a nine times greater chance of hiring a man. I still say it doesn't matter what the gender of the candidate is; we just want the best person for the job who fits with our vision, values, and culture."

"I get what you're saying, Jack. It wouldn't make much sense to try and predetermine the sex of our new hires. But I still think we'll get a much higher proportion of male applicants than female," Velma stated. "Another thing I think we should consider that we didn't put on our perfect candidate list the first time is fitness. We said someone who is a smoker is a nonstarter, but we didn't go beyond that. I think we should be looking for someone who's disciplined about his health and is physically fit. All other things being equal, we would expect that person to have less time lost due to health issues and—no disrespect Fred—no time lost due to sudden health events."

"I'm OK with it," chuckled Fred. "I'm a nonsmoker now, and I'm a whole lot more concerned about my fitness than I used to be!"

"As long as we're talking about fitness, we should also include something about presentation worthiness," said Catherine. "Whether it's Fred's or Velma's replacement, we can expect they'll be front and center when we're making project presentations. Wouldn't it be great to have someone who projects a vigorous, energetic, vibrant, and attractive image for the company? I know it might sound superficial, but what I'm saying is, I think we want someone who not only meets our requirements but also looks the part of a successful construction company executive."

"This is all terrific stuff," said Tom. "You're doing a good job fleshing out what your perfect CEO should look like."

The group went on for about a half hour debating, adding to, and amending their profile.

"Changing the subject ever so slightly," Tom intoned, "we need to talk about how to replace Velma and what that person should look like. There's been some turnover in that department, so we need to consider the company's needs in administration and finance in the larger sense, not just how we'd attempt to replace Velma as an individual. The new person, not being an owner with Velma's extensive knowledge of the company's inner workings, will probably be more focused and won't be an all-around go-to person as Velma has been for all these years. Also, Addie has left the company, and with all due respect, Amos is sixty-six years old and he'll have to be replaced sometime in the next few years. We need to think bigger picture rather than just replacing one departing vice president."

Amos grumbled something unintelligible.

Fred reached his hand across the table in Amos's direction. "OK, buddy, we're not trying to give you the bum's rush. But as we consider our long-term future, we do need to make sure we have the right staffing in key positions. You might not be thinking about retirement just now, but I wasn't either just a few months ago. We need to make sure we have our ducks in a row in the event something changes suddenly."

Amos looked down at his papers, his neck and cheeks flushing noticeably.

"That's right, Amos," said Jack. "It would be foolish for us to fail to consider our long-term needs in a vital company department. We've got to build our bench strength and allow for training time, too. There will necessarily be some overlap with Fred and Velma as we get new people up to speed."

"Our head count and payroll costs are going to skyrocket!" Amos whined. "And you said we were going to put a moratorium on all hiring just a few months ago, Tom!"

"I've been thinking about that," said Tom. "Replacing departing executives isn't the same as new hiring. And as a nonowner, it's not likely that we'd have to pay Velma's replacement the same she gets paid, so we'll actually save some money there."

He continued. "I've been thinking that what Dobach Mechanical needs as we grow is a little more firepower at the head of admin/finance. Again, no disrespect, Amos," Tom said as he looked over and found Amos glaring at him. "You've done a good job for a long time, but it might be nice to upgrade from a controller to a chief financial officer, a CFO, who can provide more guidance on budgeting, forward-looking financials, projecting cash flows, negotiating credit and deposit facilities a little more aggressively, modernizing IT, etc. A good CFO will be a godsend as our growth accelerates."

"You're just full of surprises today, Tom!" growled Larry. "I was thinking we'd be talking about finding talent to replace Fred as president and Velma as vice president, but you're talking about realigning the executive structure of the company. It might take me a little while to get my mind wrapped around all that."

"What about the rest of you?" Tom asked. "What are you thinking and feeling?"

Catherine spoke up first, "I think what you're proposing makes perfect sense. We're at a point of evaluating our future. We're on the cusp of a once-in-a-generation leadership change, so it's logical that we examine the executive structure, not for what it's done or failed to do in the past, but what it needs to do in the future. We'd be remiss if we didn't take this opportunity to consider exactly what you're proposing."

"Maybe I'm looking at things a little different now since it looks like I'm going to be the only G2 person left," said Casey. "But I'm with Catherine. We've been doing business planning, and we're learning to think strategically as a group. Therefore, analyzing what structure would best serve us in the future makes more sense than clinging to the structure we've had in the past. Boy, sometimes I can't believe I'm hearing myself say these things! The events of the past seven months have really had an effect on me!"

Everyone smiled.

"I agree one hundred percent with Catherine and Casey," Jack said decisively. "If we can get a high-powered CFO to run admin/finance and replace Aunt Velma and, eventually, Amos with just one person, it's a real no-brainer. We'll be able to have new capabilities and potentially even save some money. If it's not too forward and not too soon, I'd like to throw my hat in the ring for the CFO position. I don't think I'm nearly ready to step in for Dad and become CEO, but, given my past experience and training, I think with fairly little preparation I could do an adequate job as CFO."

"There's no reason in the world why you couldn't throw your hat in that ring, Jack." said Tom. "The real question for the SPPT—and perhaps more importantly for the Dobach family as owners—is, if Jack is going to be a candidate for CFO, do we want to undertake a nationwide search at all? Or do you have sufficient confidence in his intelligence and capabilities that you would be satisfied that he could do the job? We will have a job description for the CFO, whether it's Jack or anyone else, so we'll be able to evaluate his performance somewhat objectively. If Jack hits his targets and does all the things required of him, no problem. If, on the other hand, he doesn't measure up and we'd be better off bringing in talent from the outside, then we'll go in another direction. What do you all think?"

Velma said, "I think Jack would do a tremendous job. It seems like exactly the kind of role he's cut out for. I have no problem at all entrusting him with the CFO role."

"It would thrill me to have Jack as our new CFO!" thundered Larry. "He'll do a whale of a job!"

"Fred, Catherine, Amos? What do you three think?" asked Tom.

"I'm a little biased; maybe you should get input from the others before me," said Fred.

"Don't look at me," huffed Amos. "Leon told me to never question a family member, and I'm not about to start now!"

"We did say we wanted someone from a bigger company—don't forget about that. Having made that point, in my view Jack would be a terrific CFO!" exclaimed Catherine. "I can't imagine we'd find a candidate any more capable than Jack anywhere, and he offers the added bonus of having a commitment to the business like Aunt Velma has brought to the job. I think he has the perfect combination of attributes—although I'm sure the learning curve will be steep."

"That simplifies things, then," said Tom. "We will only have to look for one C-level executive versus two. And, Amos, that drives that budget number back down to $3,500."

Amos shot Tom a pointed look.

"Moving on, here are a couple of sample job descriptions we've used before for family business CEOs and CFOs," said Tom. "Let's take a look at these and see how we might be able to adapt them for your purposes. Jack, of course, will need some training to be able to fulfill one hundred percent of the job duties you see listed for CFO, but I don't think that will be an issue, will it Jack?"

"Absolutely not!" Jack gushed. "There are some good CFO courses I could take back at Wharton. I can pick up some real value from those!"

The SPPT focused on the information Tom had passed around.

After about an hour's discussion, Tom said, "The next thing we need to do is post the CEO ad on the various job boards. We want to use the big, famous ones to get maximum reach, but we also want to use some others that have been productive for us in the past. For example, we'll want to go out to the construction associations and use their job posting services to find people with specific industry experience. LinkedIn has been a good resource for us, too; we'll want to use that. And there are two or three others I'm considering."

"Every one of these job boards"—Amos used air quotes—"you're talking about sounds like it's going to increase the costs. Do we really need all of them? Can't we just use the biggest one and go with that?"

"Good question, Amos. It may seem redundant to use these different resources, but keep in mind that we're looking for world-class, superstar-level talent. We cannot know which source our best candidate is going to come from, so we need to spread our net as wide as possible. The more raw material we start with, the better our chances of getting just the right person in this critical job."

"Sounds like the man has a plan. I say we go with it," asserted Casey as his ample stomach growled audibly. "I'm getting hungry; when are we going to break for lunch?"

"We're almost done here. I have about all the material I need, I think. I just need the green light from you all to write up language for the ads and post them. We'll start to see applications trickle in almost immediately," Tom said.

"This is exciting! It seems thrilling to me that we will be able to go out into the talent marketplace and attract someone from a much larger company who already has the experience of being where we want to go—no disrespect to Uncle Fred or Aunt Velma, of course," said Catherine.

"It surprises me a little bit, but I find this pretty exciting myself!" said Fred. "It might be nice to transition into the roles of owner, investor, and board member without having to be up to my elbows in details every day."

"I'm way ahead of you—I've been thinking along those lines for a few months now," said Velma. "I can see how we might get the best of both worlds out of this; Fred and I will still be here to help during the transition and do whatever it takes to make sure the company is running well. But all the dirty jobs and heavy lifting will go to someone else. It's going to be liberating!"

"A few of us will have to stay around here and get the work done," rumbled Larry. "And hard work makes me hungry. Where are we going for lunch, Casey?"

XIX

November 2014

More and more we were becoming an organization comfortable with change, what one might call a "learning organization" according to Tom Hartwell. Business was strong, our backlog was continuing to grow, and we had been able to attract some super-qualified candidates to potentially replace Fred.

The Strategic Planning Project Team—now more of a hiring project team—was meeting to prepare for our first round of face-to-face interviews. The team had narrowed our list down from over three hundred to four candidates. One was within driving distance, and the others were flying in to meet with us in sequence.

Tom kicked off the meeting. "Before we get started, a couple of housekeeping issues. The first thing is, I want to say that I believe that the face-to-face, personal interview is the most flawed part of any hiring process. At the level of the candidates we're going to interview, they will all be able to discern what they think we want to hear and tell us that. In other words, they're probably going to knock your socks off with their interpersonal skills. I caution you not to get too carried away today or tomorrow."

"Second, I want you to be true to your action plan, the one you all agreed on. It would be all too easy to get excited about these interviews and quickly pull the trigger on one of the candidates. Don't be tempted! Because the personal interviews are flawed, we have built several other evaluation steps into the process, as well as a minimum of three interviews over the next month. Simply said: we won't be making any final decisions today, OK? Unfortunately, I have to give you these disclaimers because we've had clients in the past who rushed to judgment, fell in love with one of the candidates, began making lucrative offers from the get-go, and ultimately still couldn't contract with the chosen one. Because the owners had become so fixated on one particular candidate and made an immediate, lucrative offer, the other qualified candidates moved on and took other jobs. In one particular case, we never could get together with the chosen one. In fact, looking back on it, I wonder if he wasn't bargaining with our client to strengthen his hand with his old employer. We may have simply been negotiating pawns. In the end, the client was left high and dry, having wasted four months and a ton of money without the executive he so desperately needed. I would hate to see you guys make the same mistake."

"Tom, we do have a little experience hiring people around here. You may have noticed we have a couple hundred employees we found on our own without your help," stated Fred. "I would think if we feel really strongly about one of the candidates that our intuition is well developed enough where we should be free to make an offer if we so choose."

"If you all are bound and determined to make an offer to one of the candidates today, I suppose there's really no way I'd be able to stop you. However, I beg you to respect the process as fair, thorough, and objective, rather than making a leap of intuition that could prove costly. In addition, because there are eight of you on this team, there will be a need for discussion, which should allow for a thorough airing of everyone's opinions. That fact alone will probably provide a cooling off period before we pull the trigger on any one of the candidates."

"Just as long as we are clear who's in charge here—that's the point I want to make," grumbled Fred.

Gazing directly at Fred, Tom asserted evenly, "I'm one hundred percent aware of who works for whom here. I'm the sub and you guys are the GCs. But I wouldn't be providing value for you if I let you make the kind of mistake I've seen other people make in the past. My intention is not to be pushy; I just want to make sure that you guys get as close to a perfect fit as you possibly can."

Velma chimed in, turning to Fred. "I know we're tight on time, and at the risk of getting us a little off track this morning, I'd like to ask where this is coming from? For my two cents, I don't believe Tom has ever exceeded his authority or crossed any lines we may have set for him. This seems new to me, Fred, and I'd like to know if there's something bothering you?"

Fred said, "It's still early, and I guess you guys don't know it yet, but Amos came into my office this morning. He's struggled with all the changes we've made and with the level of confidence we've placed in Tom. He says he's been unhappy to the point where, when he goes home in the evenings, his wife has noticed the change. And you know Amos doesn't wear his emotions on his sleeve! They've talked quite a bit, and Amos is looking to take some time off, move down to the coast, and maybe work part-time for a smaller construction firm. He let me know he's resigning at the end of the year. I guess that's kind of bothering me. Amos has put in a quarter century here, and he and Larry are about the last two people Dad hired. I feel like I'm losing a friend, and it's got me a little bit down."

"I wondered where he was this morning; it's not like Amos to miss a meeting," said Larry.

"Wow!" intoned Velma. "Tyler, Addie, me, Fred, and now Amos! That's a lot of change in terms of the family and executive structure of our company. Maybe we need to rethink some of what we're trying to do. Are we moving too far too fast?"

"That's a great question, Velma," said Tom. "How are the rest of you feeling?"

Everyone looked around the room at one another; there was an uncomfortable silence.

Catherine looked at each of the people around the table in turn and was the first to speak up. "Everyone who has either left or intends to leave in the near future has been a terrific contributor in his or her own way. If, one year ago, you had suggested to any of us that Addie or Uncle Fred or Aunt Velma would be leaving, we'd have said you were nuts! Same goes for Amos. In a way, it's a terribly scary time for our family business; we'll blow past our record volume and profits by the end of the year, and we're still climbing. We're poised over the next three years to double in size. Coupled with that, about sixty percent of our senior leadership has intentions to leave, and leave soon. The remaining family managers—Jack, Dad, Heath, and me—represent the least experienced family contingent we've had here in a long time. That's unsettling for us as a family, and perhaps even more so for our employees and customers. From a marketing and public relations standpoint, we need to get ahead of that curve."

The others nodded in agreement.

"We as owners need to make sure everyone is reasonably comfortable with this direction. Stated succinctly, the management of Dobach Mechanical, a family-owned business sixty years old with 230 employees and over $75 million of revenue, stands to be, in a few short months' time, in the hands of a new nonfamily chief executive and a new, green CFO. That is a heckuva change!"

Again everyone nodded.

Catherine had the others spellbound with her analysis. "On the positive side of the ledger, Casey will continue as vice president of business development, and Larry will continue as General Manager. And Uncle Fred and Aunt Velma intend to stick around to smooth the transition and serve on the board. Both of those are very positive facts. In terms of kicking off the discussion, I'd like to say that I think this is the right course of action, and I'm comfortable with the changes we're making. But that's just me—what do the rest of you have to say?"

"I'm sorry to hear about Amos, too," said Larry. "I also feel like I'm losing a friend. Having said that, my opinion is that having Fred and Velma as directors will be a big help getting Jack and our new CEO established. Casey and Catherine have proven to be a tremendous business development team, so there won't be any change there in terms of the engine that's been fueling our growth. And, God willing, I'll be here for at least a few more years. Long and short, I know we're making plenty of changes plenty quickly, but I agree with Catherine that we're heading down the right path. Worst case, we screw up the hiring of a new CEO completely. If that happens, Fred can step back into his old role, at least on a temporary basis, until we're able to find the right person for the job. The downside to me just doesn't seem to be all that negative."

"I'm all in!" stated Jack succinctly. "Larry's right: Dad and Velma will be nearby whenever we need them. I suppose we could be making a huge mistake, but I don't think so. This feels right to me."

"I suppose some of this is my fault," Fred lamented. "If I hadn't been so lax and had cracked the whip a little more, we might not have gotten in trouble with the bank and bonding company, and we wouldn't be faced with having to make so many changes. If you asked me yesterday if we were heading down the right path, I probably would've said yes. And I have to admit, I'm looking forward to being able to slow down a little bit. But this thing with Amos really bothers me, and suddenly I question the entire direction we're planning. Is this really the right time to be looking for a new CEO given all the other changes we've made?"

"Velma, we've heard from everyone else. What are your thoughts?" asked Tom.

"I said I was going to be out by the end of the year, and I meant it. With all of the events around Addie's health and the decisions she's made, Arthur and I are as ready as we've ever been to slow down and make some changes. I suppose the news of Amos's imminent departure is a surprise to me too, and I worry about continuity in the finance department, but it's not so shattering to me that we need to rethink this entire strategic plan and reorganization. As I reflect, I'm a lot more tired and worn-out than I thought I was. And I bet you are, too, Fred, if you're honest with yourself." Fred nodded in agreement. "We are making a lot of changes, and as Tom has shown us time and again using the Change Model, that's never easy. But to get a handle on this organization, the growth we are experiencing, we're going to need new leadership. I'm looking forward to these interviews; these guys have run construction companies much larger than ours. They have so much to teach us! I'll echo what Jack said: I'm all in."

Tom looked around the room, making eye contact with everyone. "Any further discussion? I would say that the consensus is to continue with the interviews, to continue the search for our next chief executive, and to continue along the path of having Jack as CFO. Fred, you're the one most uncomfortable with where we stand. Do you have anything more you'd like to bring up?"

Fred, his hands folded on the table, cast his eyes downward as he spoke. "I guess not. Maybe I'm just an old maid worrying over nothing. And you are right in the sense that Tom has educated us every step of the way about the Change Model and the strong emotions associated with changes. Like I say, maybe Amos's announcement this morning just caught me flat-footed. I don't think we should cancel our interviews or anything like that. I was just voicing my concern that maybe the rate of change has been a little too speedy."

"That's perfectly understandable, Fred," Tom said. "Why don't we take a ten-minute break, so everyone can stretch and get a breath of air, and then we'll get the first interview started. We have two today and two more tomorrow, so they'll be long days.

In addition to the interviews themselves, we will need to debrief after each one and then have a longer debrief tomorrow to score the candidates and plan for the next steps. Let's adjourn for a few minutes."

Everyone gathered up their materials, coffee cups, and water bottles, and made their way out of the room.

As they rounded the corner, Jack caught up with Catherine as she juggled and organized her ever-present stack of books. "Way to go! I thought Dad's misgivings may have put the kibosh on this new CEO hire. I must say, I'm pretty excited about it. I love my dad and he's done a great job running the company, but we need a different level of thinking for the different future we're planning."

"Thanks, Jack. Nobody seemed to be stepping up to the plate, so I thought I would break the ice. I felt pretty lonely there, to tell you the truth! I had no idea what the consensus was or where I stood relative to anyone else. I said my part, and then I was terrified, as the youngest person in the room, that I had made a huge mistake!"

"Well, as usual, your instincts were one hundred percent sound. Not only did you do the right thing, but I think you helped everyone else feel confident that our thinking has been sound up to this point and our way is clear. You're the man, Catherine!" Jack said as he playfully punched her on the shoulder. They both laughed and headed for the kitchen for fresh bottles of water.

Over the course of the two days, the four candidates spent about two hours each with the hiring team discussing résumés, asking questions about Dobach Mechanical and the direction of the company, and answering questions about experiences and capabilities.

At the end of the second day, the group gathered as the rays of the late November sun slanted in through the blinds. "I see you squinting; let me close these so we can see one another while we wrap up the first round of face-to-face interviews," said Tom.

"Except for the last guy, they blew me away!" enthused Casey. "I thought I knew a lot about running a mechanical contracting company, but these guys made me feel like a kid! They talked infinitely more about finance and people management than I thought they would. As far as executing work in the field, it almost seems like that was an afterthought. Is that really what it takes to run a company once volume gets to be a few hundred million dollars?"

Tom shrugged his shoulders noncommittally. "What do the rest of you all think?"

"First, none of the four people would be worth a crap in the field," Larry's deep voice rumbled. "But that's not what a CEO does, is it? They were pretty impressive in how they talked about leading and inspiring people. They almost made it sound too easy: if you get the right people on the team, everything just falls into place. It can't be as simple as that, can it?"

"Of course it's not," Jack responded. "But every successful team, whether in business or in sports, breaks things down to the basics, the most fundamental parts. I think that's what these folks were getting at. We need to make sure we have mastered the basics of getting the right people on the bus, managing them effectively, measuring their performance and holding them accountable, and paying strict attention to our finances. I forget who said it, but I remember hearing that commercial construction is pretty simple. You get work, you execute work, and you keep score. If our CEO can get the people he wants and do those three fundamental things, we'll be successful for a long time to come!"

"Funny that Casey was least impressed with the fourth one. I thought he was pretty darn good," said Velma. "Given that there are seven of us here with roughly equally weighted opinions, how are we going to go about cutting these four down to one, Tom?"

"Excellent segue!" Tom said brightly. "Based on the discussions we had about the perfect candidate, I've come up with a scorecard we can use to come to a consensus opinion about our applicants." Tom passed the scorecard matrix around the table. "As you can see, we've listed the attributes from the perfect candidate model. I'd like for you to rate our four candidates, three men and one woman, on each attribute on a scale of one to ten. Just go with your own opinion; don't worry what others in the group are thinking. We'll discuss that in a few minutes. Let's just do a quick and dirty exercise to see if we can neatly come up with a consensus."

"Is this anything like electing a new pope?" joked Casey.

"Almost," replied Tom, smiling. They concentrated on the scorecards, with jaw muscles flexing, lips pursed, and pens scribbling rapidly. After about ten minutes, it appeared that all were finished.

"Let's see what you guys came up with. Why don't we take a break while I tabulate these answers, and then we'll reconvene and see if there's a clear direction," Tom instructed.

The group broke up amid the chatter and scraping of chairs.

Once they had reassembled, Tom walked through the evaluation results on his ubiquitous easel pad. He had written the interviewees' names across the top and listed the perfect candidate attributes along the left side. Each candidate's average score was filled in on the appropriate line, with the cumulative scores at the bottom of the page. Tom asked for everyone's attention: "It looks like the two middle candidates, Jonathan and Doug, got the highest average scores by a pretty fair margin. Does that surprise anyone? Let's have a bit of discussion."

"I'm not surprised," Velma asserted. "I didn't agree with Casey, necessarily, on the last candidate, but I think the group's sense of Doug and Jonathan looks about right. They both have loads of experience running mechanical contracting companies or large divisions, and I like the way both of them focus on the use of rigorous people and financial measurement tools. I think if we got either one of these guys, we'd be very lucky. I guess I am a little disappointed that our only female candidate didn't score a little better!"

Jack spoke up. "We ought to be scrupulously fair. Do we need to rethink the scores we gave Elizabeth? I don't want to even give the appearance that, because she's a woman, she didn't have at least as good a chance as everyone else."

"I'm not at all worried about that, Jack. I was just joking a little bit," said Velma. "Catherine, do you think these evaluations are fair?"

"Absolutely. My feeling is that we gave her the exact same chance we gave the others, and there was no gender bias whatsoever in our preliminary selection of the two finalists. I wouldn't give it another thought."

Fred and Casey spoke up at almost the same time. "Go ahead, Casey," Fred said.

"I was just going to say that I think I can be happy with either one of these guys. They're both as impressive as they can be. When can we make an offer?" Tom gave Casey a surprised look, and Casey burst out in a big smile. "Gotcha, Tom! I was listening; don't get your feathers in a ruffle!"

Tom laughed, along with the rest of the group.

"For my part, I agree with where we are," Fred stated. "Let's continue down the path with Jonathan and Doug. Tom, are you going to take care of notifying the other two?"

"Not just yet, Fred," Tom advised. "I don't want to come off as mercenary here, but let's not let any of these folks off the hook just yet. On the outside chance that we can't get together with either Doug or Jonathan, we might want to keep these two in reserve as a backup. As soon as we think we're in the clear with respect to our top two, I'll give them a heads-up so they can move on to other opportunities. I'm sure they're both very much in demand."

"That sounds good to me," Fred concurred.

"You said the personal interview is the most flawed part of the hiring process, Tom. What comes next?" inquired Catherine.

"Great question! The next thing we want to do, if you refer to your action plan, is to do some psychological profiling and, in addition, give them skills assessments."

"A skills assessment?" inquired Velma. "You have got to be kidding! We're not hiring a typist; we can't measure words per minute or software proficiency with people like this. What exactly are we going to assess?"

"We're going to try to get some insight into their thinking as entrepreneurial business people," Tom said evenly. "I agree that hiring an executive doesn't parallel very neatly with hiring a typist or a plumber. What we're going to do, however, is give them a very challenging open-ended assignment. With your permission, I'd like to give them five years of financials through the end of 2013."

"Don't you mean 2014 year-to-date, Tom?" asked Fred.

"No, I think for our purposes 2013 will be fine. What we want to see is either Jonathan's or Doug's insight into the financial health of the company before things got to the point where the bank and bonding company began to wave red flags. I'd like to have them give us a written report of their observations and what actions they would have taken in order to arrest the decline of the financials and put Dobach Mechanical back on even ground."

"That sounds good!" Jack stated.

"One more thing," Tom continued. "I'd also like for them to present at least one complete business plan they've developed for a previous employer. Of course, I'll ask them to take out names or anything else that could be considered a breach of confidentiality. I'll feel a lot better seeing a strategic plan they've put together rather than just nodding my head in agreement when they say it's one of their core capabilities. As Ronald Reagan once said, 'Trust but verify.'"

Catherine piped up. "Tom, shouldn't we open it up a bit in order to allow each of them to put their best foot forward? In other words, suppose they've developed business tools over the years of which they are extremely proud. Maybe they have created something unusually predictive or productive. Even with all your travels, there have to still be things even you're not aware of."

"Terrific idea, Catherine!" Tom exclaimed. "I love that! Thanks for the idea. I should've thought of it myself, but I knew I could count on you."

Catherine smiled in appreciation, and Casey beamed as only a proud father could.

"Folks, you should be very satisfied with yourselves. You have had a most productive couple of days. Fred's questioning our direction was perfectly valid, and I thank him for that. It's always good to undertake a sanity check before taking a big planning step. I also thank you for coming to consensus so quickly. You're all quite comfortable with embracing change now and seeing it not as a negative but as the opportunity it so often really is. In fact, I think after this hiring project is done that I have about worked myself out of a job!"

An uneasiness rippled throughout the room. "Don't be so hasty, Tom!" Jack said. "You've been a real Catalyst." Tom smiled at Jack's choice of words, having come directly from the Change Model. "And we've come to depend on your thinking and steady hand. This is just my opinion, and I don't mean to speak for the rest of the group, but we've gotten our money's worth with you and your firm."

Heads around the table nodded in assent.

"Don't worry, I'm not going to abandon you midproject," Tom reassured everyone. "But at some point every good consultant works himself out of a job, and I think I might be nearing that point with you all. What we might consider doing is transitioning to a quarterly type of meeting schedule instead of me being here for few days each month. Especially as you get a new chief executive on board, he's going to need to be free to assist the family in charting this new direction without me looking over his shoulder all the time!"

"We'll talk about that once we have the new man on board, Tom," said Fred. "Right now, I think everybody's tired after a productive session. Why don't we call it a day?"

The group wearily gathered up their belongings and made their way for the door.

XX

February 2015

Fred, Velma, Jack, Heath, Catherine, Larry, and the new CEO Doug McHenry were gathering with consultant Tom Hartwell for a business meeting.

"How is 'retirement,' Aunt Velma?" asked Jack.

"I have to say, I'm loving it more than even I thought I would!" Velma replied. "No fires to put out, no employee headaches, no deadlines to worry about, no bank or bonding company to upset me when I'm not expecting it, and—no disrespect to anybody in this room—no family dynamics to worry about when Arthur and I want to make a spending decision or just go to the beach. The only downside is that I'm having to make new friends at the gym because I'm not going at six in the morning anymore!"

Fred said, "You make it sound too good to be true! Now that Doug has been on board for a couple of months, I'm looking forward to spending less time at the office, too!"

Doug spoke up. "I'm not quite ready for you to ride off into the sunset, Fred. There are still quite a few things I'm learning about from you. I don't feel as if I'm trying to take a sip of water from a fire hose anymore, but there are still a host of items to check off our list. You might have a little more freedom by the time spring rolls around."

"I can't wait! I'm confident I'm leaving the company in capable hands. We made a great selection bringing you on board! You've already made a difference."

"Hear, hear!" exclaimed Jack, with the nodding approval of those around the conference table.

"Now that we're all present and accounted for, why don't we get down to business?" asked Catherine. "Tom, are you ready?"

"Absolutely! What we need to be planning for now is strategy to cover the next three years on a rolling basis. Much of what we did for the bank back in the spring of last year was, frankly, work that I produced on your behalf. Never having done comprehensive strategic planning before, you needed me to do most of the heavy lifting. Now we need to make sure that you guys, by yourselves, are in a position to continue the process of thinking about and planning for the business so you don't lose any of the hard-earned momentum you've established."

"Boy! It's just one thing after another," Casey groaned. "Since you've been here, Tom, I feel like I don't have any time to do the day-to-day stuff! We're always working on a hiring plan or a strategic plan or something. The one we prepared for the bank and bonding company was through 2017. Can't we just use that one and wait a year or two before we go about reinventing the wheel?"

"Great question, Casey. Let me see if I can answer that—"

"Mind if I take a stab at this one, Tom?" asked Catherine.

"Not at all!" Tom replied. Catherine had become more and more outspoken and assertive in the group's meetings. She seemed to be finding her confidence, and the group clearly respected her insights.

Catherine began by passing around a sheet of paper with a colorful graphic. "Since we embarked on this process last year, I've been doing a lot of reading on the subject of corporate strategic planning, and I put together this graphic to help illustrate what I've gleaned as a planning best practice. Subject to the group's approval and some editing, I'd like to move that we adopt an annual strategic planning cycle like this one so that we stay ahead of the curve."

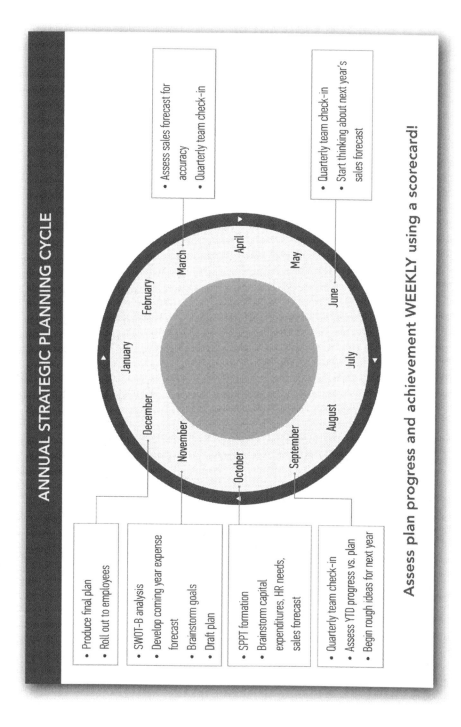

ANNUAL STRATEGIC PLANNING CYCLE

- Assess sales forecast for accuracy
- Quarterly team check-in

- Quarterly team check-in
- Start thinking about next year's sales forecast

- Produce final plan
- Roll out to employees

- SWOT-B analysis
- Develop coming year expense forecast
- Brainstorm goals
- Draft plan

- SPPT formation
- Brainstorm capital expenditures, HR needs, sales forecast

- Quarterly team check-in
- Assess YTD progress vs. plan
- Begin rough ideas for next year

January, February, March, April, May, June, July, August, September, October, November, December

Assess plan progress and achievement WEEKLY using a scorecard!

"In answer to Dad's question, strategic planning is a dynamic process that is really never ending. The mistake I think many small businesses make is that they do long-term planning at the behest of a bank or other outsider, get a nice narrative and *pro forma* financials together, stuff it all in a pretty three-ring binder, and then put it on a shelf while breathing a huge sigh of relief and returning to business as usual. They don't see that the value of the plan is in the process itself: the process of pulling together the best brains in the company, establishing a common vision, debating the pros and cons of this action versus that one, etc. Don't you get it? It's the process that has value for us! That's why we're suddenly out of the woods and pulling together in one direction as a team!

"As far as I'm concerned, I don't ever want to go back to 'business as usual.' Instead of getting a scary call from the bank that throws us all into a tizzy, I'd rather take the things we've learned from Tom, make them our own, and build on them for the benefit our family company. The catalysts that have fueled our growth and momentum over the past few months have been Tom and the strategic planning process he introduced to us. Now that he is cutting back to quarterly visits—"

There were some concerned glances around the table.

"We need to be assured that we're competent to continue the planning process. One has only to look at our revenue, profits, and backlog to see that we're on to something. And if we were going to drop the strategic planning ball, why did we put such an emphasis on long-term planning during the process of evaluating and hiring Doug?" Catherine concluded.

"So, looking at this graphic, Catherine, you're saying strategic planning is an ongoing process if we're going to do it right. Is that correct?" inquired Jack.

"That's exactly what I'm saying." Catherine looked at Tom and Doug, who were vigorously nodding their agreement.

"You mean to tell me we're going to be getting together five or six times a year to review this thing? When are we going to have time to do everything else we're supposed to do? We were successful for a long time without doing this kind of stuff; is the pendulum swinging too far?" Casey asked.

Doug stepped up to the plate. "I love this discussion and where Catherine is going. In fact, if she hadn't produced a graphic like this one, I would have. One of the things that separates a company like Dobach Mechanical, which is experiencing rapid growth in a relatively slow growth environment, is senior management's ability and willingness to take time to work *on* the business versus just working *in* it. If you are interested in going back to the way you used to do things—before the bank fired a shot across your bow and before Tom got involved—you don't need me, and you don't need to do big-picture planning like this. On the other hand, if you want to expand your beachhead and extend your gains, this is exactly the kind of corporate planning muscle you need to develop. The devil is in the details, and we will always have to make sure we're paying attention to project execution. But the thing that will drive your continued growth and prosperity is refining your vision, getting the best quality people, and creating a business plan that will pave the way for you to hit your targets."

Tom Hartwell was bursting with enthusiasm. "Casey, does that answer your question?" he asked.

"I suppose so. Looking at the Change Model"—Casey fished a copy of the model out of his stack of notes—"I guess I was making the mistake of getting a little uncomfortable and trying to rush back to the old Status Quo, huh?"

"You guys are a consultant's dream!" exclaimed Tom. "To hear you use the language I've tried to teach you about the Change Model, strategic planning, getting the right people on the bus, and working on the business versus working in it just warms my heart! I hope you all have gotten as much out of this assignment as I have! I can't imagine being any prouder of a family business!"

"Come on, Tom! This is getting a little sappy and embarrassing! What happened to the stern, fast-paced, all-business consultant we hired last year?" Fred intoned.

"Maybe I am getting a little sappy. I'm going to miss you when I'm not here every month. Well, I guess we ought to get back to work."

With that, the group began to brainstorm high-level priorities for 2016 and beyond.

Toward the end of the day, Tom brought up a new item. "Remember when we got started last year we did a survey of almost everyone in the company to gather some quantifiable data about morale and other things? A couple of weeks ago, we recirculated the survey to see if we had moved the needle. Please have a look at this." Tom passed around the new survey results for everyone to see. "Whether family members, as you can see in the separate table, or employees, the scores have gone up pretty dramatically. I know this isn't a perfect, scientific survey, but you ought to feel really happy about the things you've done and the progress you've made."

Looking at the scores, Larry said, "This *is* an improvement! I guess I had forgotten how low morale had sunk. We thought it was normal, maybe just a part of our culture or industry that people were unhappy or disgruntled. We just took the bitching and moaning for granted. We took lots of things for granted. I do feel good about this; I think there's as much excitement about Dobach Mechanical as I can ever remember!"

"I think so, too, Larry. Maybe in Dad's early days, when the company was experiencing its first real growth and becoming a presence, things were this good, but we really are at a new place," stated Velma. "Tom, are you sure that this has nothing to do with my retirement? Is that why everybody is so pleased?" she asked, smiling.

"If that's the case, the reading will be off the charts in a few months when I leave!" chuckled Fred.

"I guess the only thing that can make things better would be for me to hit the road, too!" Casey boomed.

Looking at Catherine and Jack, Doug said, "If this keeps up, we're going to be the last ones left!"

"Before we break up, I'd like to show you one more graphic I put together." Catherine passed around another composition. "My goal here was to try and contrast, as best I could, the way things were when we had our bank meeting almost a year ago versus where we stand today. I'm not trying to blow Tom's horn, but as we begin to wind down this aspect of our project, I wanted everyone to see another indication of how far we've come."

Looking at Catherine's document, Jack said, "Boy, this is like one of those before and after diet ads with the overweight guy on one side and the muscular stud on the other." There were a few chuckles. "To extend my analogy, we were pretty flabby a year ago! And we have made an amazing transformation as a family business!"

"Tom, did you put Catherine up to or help her with this?" asked Fred.

"Not at all! This is all Catherine!"

She said, "We're certainly not ready to rest on our laurels, but I thought it would be a real positive for us to have a before and after snapshot. We probably, as a family and a business, don't stop and appreciate and celebrate our successes enough. We're always worried about where we fell short or what we didn't quite do perfectly, but when you look at how far we've come in a short amount of time, you can't help but feel a swell of pride and accomplishment. I'd like for us to measure our incremental progress better and celebrate our small victories. After all, it's a series of small accomplishments that lead to bigger ones."

"This is outstanding work, Catherine." said Larry.

FAMILY BUSINESS PLANNING

Business	BEFORE	AFTER
	Lack of common vision	Defined business vision
	Misunderstood family business roles	• Differentiated unique roles of owner/manager/BOD
		• Defined roles of outside directors(s)/role of board
	No defined growth targets for the various business entities	Growth expectations set for each
	No defined geographic expansion plan	Defined (where, how, when) expansion plans
	No future organization structure	Worked on what the future company must look like in order to achieve future goals
	"Blindsiding" communication habits	Delivered specifics on "who needs what info when and how" to prevent anyone being blindsided
	Desire for family harmony made business decisions difficult due to unanimity rules over even modest choices	• Moved "unanimous" governance requirements to super majority
		• "Moved" unanimous" governance requirements from buy-sell and corporate bylaws
	Family based compensation (equal pay)	Changed compensation from all same to market
	Disagreement over company valuation(s)	Clarified stock valuation
	Little understanding of differing unique personalities and related wishes/needs	Psychographic instruments to improve communication and acceptance of differences
	Low self awareness and related management blind spots	360-degree evaluations and related coaching
	Little delegation among senior leaders	Improved delegation capabilities
	Doing	Mentoring, teaching, and transitioning
	Buy-sell agreements not in place for all entities	Buy-sell improvements and new buy-sell documents are in process
	Communication among family and from family executives was mostly of the "ass-chewing" variety	Transitioned feedback to more of the "pat on the back" variety
	Job performance evaluations mailed to employees	One-to-one in-depth reviews of division managers/executives
	Infrequent interaction of senior management with rank-and-file employees	• Employee surveys
		• "Lottery Lunches" to provide employees access to company president and vice versa

FAMILY BUSINESS PLANNING

	BEFORE	AFTER
Family	No structured, mutually agreed upon means for the large family to coordinate and communicate	• Created family council and related structure • Family vision and values statement • Opened lines of communication between family and business and vice versa with mutual reporting • Monthly participation from all family branches • Orchestrated volunteering • Planned family vacations • Video about Gobach family values budgeted
	Poorly defined family/relationship roles	Define roles within context of family council
	Low trust; infrequent, unstructured communication	• Eliminated hearsay and misunderstandings • Budget for family council (in process) funded by family business • Psychographic instruments to improve communication and acceptance of differences • Reconnected business family to non-employee family (and NextGen of both varieties) • Offered tools to combat trust breakdowns and how to self-diagnose low trust situations
Next-generation owners	No definition of criteria for future ownership	Specific prerequisites to be eligible for ownership
Drop Dead Plans	Some had no wills, all dated	Reviews and updates (as necessary) in process
Gifts	$ and type in dispute	Coordinated (up to) $5.12 mil UTC gifts
Testamentary Trusts	Basic, revocable	State-of-the-art, irrevocable
Stock	All S Corp voting	1:9 split voting to nonvoting while maintaining S-Corp status
Death Tax 10 Year Savings	n/a	$900,000 to $4,500,000 per sibling
Board of Directors	Few formal governance rules	Clearly articulated rules for governance
	No outside directors	Defined need and criteria for outside directors

Everyone else gave Catherine "attaboys" as well. Jack looked at his cousin and smiled proudly.

Doug asked, "Why don't we do exactly that, Catherine? If you'll agree to be our chief morale officer, I think the group would be very happy to have you periodically assess our progress. You know the old saying about a journey of one thousand miles begins with—"

"If that's what the group wants me to do, I'm happy to add it to my list of duties. And I assume as chief morale officer that any other clever ideas I come up with along these lines will also be part of my portfolio, right?"

Doug said, "That's exactly right! As long as the rest of the team is in agreement."

The group gave their blessings.

Tom said, "That's about it for today, unless someone else has a surprise for us. If that's not the case, we will convene back here bright and early in the morning to continue improving the Dobach Mechanical strategic plan. Thanks, everyone!"

January 2034

Dobach Mechanical has sustained its growth and driven change initiatives aggressively over the past twenty years. From a 2014 starting place of financial frailty, uncertainty, and a lack of clear direction, our company has evolved into a regional powerhouse doing over $500 million a year. And the Dobach family has changed quite a bit, too...

The last twenty years have been a blur! So many changes, so many opportunities, so many people...it's hard to imagine that two decades have passed since the First National meeting that so rattled us. In hindsight, the bank did us a favor by snapping us out of our somnambulant status quo and causing us to seek out new tools and talent to restore the entrepreneurial spirit with which Leon had created his business.

Myra lived to be ninety-three. Her dementia progressed, and by the end, she recognized neither Fred nor Velma. Casey seemed to bring out the best in her; until she passed, she still recognized and responded to him almost as if his oversized personality were a miracle cure that could wash away the ravages of time.

Fred, in spite of his commitment to a healthier lifestyle, continued to have heart and respiratory problems. After his third heart attack in 2018, he resigned completely from the family business, not even keeping his seat on the board. He died in his sleep in 2020 at age seventy-two. Some think his feelings of guilt over the fact that the family business's gravest threat came on his watch accelerated his health problems and shortened his life. Fred confessed to Daphne that he felt he had let Leon and the rest of the family down, and jeopardized the family business by not being a better manager and leader.

Daphne is a healthy eighty-four years old and remarried a few years ago. Much to her delight, Dobach Mechanical opened an office near Atlanta, and Tyler came back into the family business. His time away had helped him mature, get better organized, and become the kind of man we knew he could be. He remarried—to a girl Daphne very much approved of—and had two children. Tyler is a very valuable part of the Georgia operation, is active on the SPPT, and eagerly participates in family council meetings.

Velma and Arthur, both eighty-two years old, spend most of their time at the coast. Velma still enthusiastically assists in planning family council meetings and activities. Myra worried that the family wouldn't connect outside of the business after she passed away; Velma's devotion to developing and sustaining the family council put structure and focus into place to ensure that her mother's fears wouldn't materialize. Arthur reads and spends his days on his fishing boat. He hasn't practiced law in years, and he says he doesn't miss it one bit.

Casey is seventy-nine years old and in poor health. His lifestyle and refusal to take heed of doctor's warnings of the seriousness of diabetes cost him his left foot. Amber divorced him as his health problems began to accelerate, and while he hasn't remarried, he does have a devoted companion who cares about him a great deal and attends to his needs. His legacy in the company is that Dobach Mechanical is second to none in its business development capabilities. And Generations Real Estate, the Florida property that was an albatross around the business's neck, grew just as Casey believed it would. In fact, it created so much equity the family was able to leverage the asset to acquire more real estate. Heath Hannah, Casey's son-in-law, had shown interest and talent in the real estate business, and he heads up the small team that runs Generations as a separate family business entity. Heath and Libbie are still happily married.

Catherine became president of the company at the age of forty and, upon Doug's retirement, became CEO as well. In addition to the improvements the company made with Tom Hartwell's firm, one of the smartest moves they made was joining a peer group of noncompeting mechanical contractors. The peer group has been instrumental in challenging Catherine and Jack to continue to stay on the cutting edge and not get complacent. They learned the hard way that it's all too easy to rest on your laurels and be lulled into complacency by a seductive status quo!

Jack is terrific in his role as CFO. He is a voracious learner, studies constantly, and innovates relentlessly. He took Dobach's financial forecasting capabilities to a new level and is so good at it that other construction companies often ask him for consulting. He and Angie set up a small consulting firm so they could cherry pick certain opportunities and help other companies improve their finance and IT capabilities, too.

Addie paid back the company every dime she took. She never really forgave herself for her transgressions—although the rest of the family certainly did. She began missing family council meetings, and her children reported that she had begun to gain weight, smoke, and live like a hermit again. In spite of Velma's and the rest of the family's best efforts, Addie took her own life at the age of forty-nine.

Allen Eastman became the CEO of his family's gasoline and convenience store business. He engineered a sale to a much larger company, and he sagely held on to the real estate. The transaction created almost $100 million of wealth for his family, and he and Lisa spend much of their time traveling among their three homes and seeking business opportunities for themselves and their children.

Larry Brown retired from the company when he turned seventy-five years old. He still came into the office about once a week, and his presence was always welcome. He spent most of his time playing golf, hunting, and fishing. He passed away in 2020, the same year as Fred, never having fully recovered from the effects of an auto accident. People said his funeral was the biggest they had ever attended. Friends, family, business associates, and even friendly competitors mourned the death of a universally admired man.

Amos Lee left Dobach Mechanical at the end of 2014 and took a job as controller with a smaller firm in Tidewater Virginia. At first he called Fred to check in from time to time, but the calls gradually ceased. No one knows exactly what became of Amos.

Tom Hartwell, the catalyst of the Dobach family business metamorphosis, worked with us on a quarterly basis for a number of years. He then introduced a younger member of his consulting company to us and handed the ball off to him. Their firm still meets with us on a semiannual basis and is instrumental in helping us refine our strategic planning and thinking. Hartwell introduced us to the Change Model, and we still use it today along with many of the other concepts he helped us develop. He also helped us add Doug McHenry to the team, and Doug was instrumental in both engineering growth and helping us refine our business model and capabilities. He retired in 2028 and still serves on the board.

While the kind of stress, uncertainty, and crises we at Dobach Mechanical endured was no one's idea of an opportunity, it did turn out that way. The hard knocks education paid dividends. We realized that our family business—almost any family business really could rally together, seek expert advice, implement positive changes, and emerge from a crisis stronger as both family and business. Our chaos helped us grow, and we continue to apply lessons learned to engineer a better family and a better business.

Made in the USA
Middletown, DE
01 February 2018